P9-CQI-245

Poul Borchsenius, the famous Danish Lutheran pastor, is celebrated for two reasons. He played a noble part in the Danish resistance to the Nazis, and was the hero of a scheme to save the Jews of Jutland in 1943. He is sometimes affectionately termed ''the shooting priest''. Pastor Borchsenius is also one of the world's leading Christian exponents of Judaism and most of his books (which include THE THREE RINGS, a history of Spanish Jewry: THE SON OF A STAR, on Bar Kochba; THE CHAINS ARE BROKEN, the story of Jewish emancipation) demonstrate his passionate belief in the affinity between his own faith and that of the Jews. In 1964, under the auspices of B'nai B'rith, he lectured extensively in England and America. He lives in Randers, Denmark.

TWO WAYS TO GOD

POUL BORCHSENIUS

TWO WAYS TO GOD

JUDAISM AND CHRISTIANITY

Translated from the Danish by
MICHAEL HERON

FOREWORD BY THE REV.
THE LORD SOPER

VALLENTINE : MITCHELL / LONDON

SBN: 85303 011 1

First published under the title
'To Veje' by H. Hirschprungs Forlag, Copenhagen

First published in Great Britain 1968 by
Vallentine, Mitchell & Co. Ltd.
18 Cursitor Street, London, E.C.4

© 1968 Vallentine, Mitchell & Co. Ltd.
© To Veje: Poul Borchsenius.

Printed and bound in Great Britain by
Northumberland Press Limited, Gateshead.

CONTENTS

45341

FOREWORD

IT WOULD BE A PRIVILEGE TO WRITE A FORE-
word to this book, if for no other reason than to
commend to English readers Poul Borchsenius—a
Danish pastor who is its author. A man famous in his own
country, it is probable that comparatively few know of him in
these islands. This is their loss and a matter to be remedied. Poul
Borchsenius is a conspicuous religious figure in Denmark, but his
fame is already established in a wider context. He played an outstanding and courageous part in helping to save Denmark's Jews
during the occupation. I understand that a film about him is in
preparation. When therefore he writes a book, as this one is, about
Judaism and Christianity, his own life is the vital context in
which its purpose and message are set. 'Two Ways to God' deals
with an urgently contemporary theme with its roots far back in
the history book, and its relevance as up-to-date as this morning.
It may well be that there are others like myself who have deplored
in our life-time the lack of intelligent attention which has been
given to the relationship between Judaism and Christianity. All
too much has been written and said about the traditional anti-
thesis between the two religions, and most of it superficial and
unscholarly. For long enough the Jewish people have lain under
the unwarrantable accusation of deicide; in fact, the preoccupa-
tion with the particular rejection of the claims of Jesus by official
Jewry has obscured the wider field of mutual relationship, and
much worse, has contributed to bitterness and contumely. The
theme, however, of these two thousand years of controversy and
misunderstanding is not an easy one to embark upon. It requires
a dispassionate quality of mind, and an equally charitable approach. It demands scholarship of an exact order, and above all a
dedication to the religious spirit of man at its highest and noblest.
It is not a fulsome compliment to say that it is with these qualities
admirably blended that this book is undertaken. Let me quote
the author's own words, as he sets out the work to which he
addresses himself—

'Here is the crux of everything that this book has to say. We
see two religions confronting each other both of which sprang
from the same root and profess one God, the Creator, the
Redeemer, and bow to His holy will. And this one almighty
God chose Israel as His people. He revealed himself and

made a covenant with them. Israel needs no one else and has clung to Him for thousands of years. But this same living God led its history by winding ways so that in the middle of it—we Christians say "in the fulness of time"—He gave His Son to redeem us through suffering and death; He raised Him from the dead and made a new covenant with the world. Israel said "no" to it and the church "yes"; the two parted and God's one way became two ways which eventually ran far apart.'

In language which is at once moving and measured the various chapters expound this theme, and set it within the context of the world which surrounded, and from time to time lorded it over the people of the Jews. It is no intention of mine to attempt a digest of the book. I would, however, offer two reasons for which any scholar or interested person should be grateful for it. The author has never been inhibited from appreciating the qualities of the Jewish faith for fear that such an appreciation might reflect unfavourably upon his commitment to Christianity. His approach is inclusive rather than divisive, and therefore his entire attitude is instinct with hope—'the two ways which eventually ran apart' are not of necessity to be permanently divergent. There is no bleak 'either—or'.

The other characteristic which I find impressive is the brief but cogent presentation of the inter-testamental period which goes so far to explain the precise conditions in which the critical clash between Jesus and the Pharisees, Pauline and later Jewish thought, the primitive church and the dispersed Jewish community, took place.

'Two Ways to God' pretends to no easy conclusion and wisely avoids any neat programme of reconciliation. The author is content to offer an adventure in faith for both Jew and Christian. In fact a mutual understanding of the Ways of God to man as expressed in the Jewish covenant and the Christian Gospel leads Poul Borchsenius to the cautious but optimistic conclusion that—

'difficult times will teach synagogue and church to look ahead to the things that are to come. Here in any case is what unites them and helps them to come closer together. After all, they are both waiting for one who is to come, the Jews for Messiah, the Christians for the return of Jesus, and the two are the same person. Jews and Christians can pray together: "Thy kingdom come".'

If such a book as this can help to bring that realm nearer it was infinitely worth writing and deserves to be read by everyone who yearns to see the 'Kingdoms of this world become the Kingdoms of Our God'.

London, 1968   Soper

1 / TWO PICTURES

ABOUT SIX MILES NORTH OF RANDERS, A
town in Jutland, lies an old country village
called Spentrup. The church at Spentrup is old;
it was erected 800 years ago during the great building period
under the Waldemars. It had not been standing very long
when an otherwise unknown artist painted a picture on the
triumphal arch that opens up the choir to the congregation.
Like most holy pictures from the age of Catholicism, it was
painted over when the gale of the Reformation swept the
Danish church. But a little less than a hundred years ago the
picture began to show through the plaster and has now been
uncovered and restored. Once seen, this picture is never
forgotten. Every time I have stood in front of it, its primitive
yet elegant beauty has fascinated me. Its creator was a first-
class artist and he was outstanding technically as well. He
painted in natural colours of lamp-black, ochre, vermilion
and verdigris, but he also used the priceless blue that is ob-
tained from lapis lazuli. The picture has withstood the ravages
of time. Even if some of the colours have faded, we see it
today as the congregation saw it for centuries before it was
painted over.

The top of the painting is dominated by the lamb, *Agnus
Dei*, the lamb of God, the symbol of Christ, taken from Isaiah
53, about the Suffering Servant of the Lord, who was
'wounded for our transgressions . . . yet he opened not his
mouth: he is brought as a lamb to the slaughter'. Underneath
the lamb stand two beautiful young women. The woman on

the left has flowing hair over her green skirt; the woman on the right wears a queen's dress under her scarlet coat. The two women are the synagogue and the church. The synagogue has a bandage over her eyes; we read in St. Paul (II Corinthians 3: 15) that 'even unto this day, when Moses is read, the veil is upon their (the Jews') hearts'. She does not see that Jesus is the Saviour. The woman holds a lance; she pushes it up into the lamb's throat, inflicting a fatal wound. Blood spurts from the wound, but the church catches the streaming blood in a chalice. So the crown falls from the synagogue's head, while the church tramples victoriously on the snake's head, fulfilling the prophecy that woman's seed shall crush its head.

The blindfolded synagogue murders Our Saviour and loses her crown. The church, regally beautiful and victorious, collects the sacrificial blood. This is the medieval church's picture of the two religions. The theme is by no means unique. It can also be found in famous churches throughout the old Christian countries of Europe. There is a celebrated picture of the same two women in Strasbourg Cathedral. But so established and widespread was the church's view of the synagogue's unbelief and punishment that a remote village church in Denmark bears witness to it, and Sunday after Sunday its congregation has been indoctrinated with the idea that the Jews murdered Christ and that the church inherited Israel's place in the story of the Redemption.

The picture seems to emit an echo of uneasiness; it expresses the unrest, indeed the *angst*, of the early church at the mere thought of the Jews and the eternal problem they raised by simply existing. And even when we tear ourselves away from the picture of the two women, they vibrate in our minds long after we have left the church. We have stood face to face with an enigma that is as old as the Christian church.

Two thousand years ago the church broke loose from the synagogue; the one way to God split into two, and since then they have moved far apart. When Israel said 'No' to the gospel, God's people were disrupted and an abyss of mutual distrust and prejudice gaped between synagogue and church.

The fact that it could happen is incomprehensible, and even though no man born of woman is able to fathom the depths of this mystery, the church must never stop pondering over it. For never has a knife cut so deep and so painfully as then; an ever-open wound still bleeds from it.

The thought of unbelieving Israel has always haunted the church like a nightmare. Even during its earliest years the church was astonished that the majority of the Jewish people rejected the gospel. And when it became a world power and Europe's barbarian people bowed before the Christ, there was one people, one single people, that stubbornly kept themselves apart and clung steadfastly to their traditional faith; the Jews remained Jews. The church felt insecure whenever its thoughts so much as touched on these obdurate nay-sayers. It also felt that they might become dangerous. Even though they were few and their synagogues mean and shabby, unbelief was fostered by the sight of men denying the Church's central doctrines and nevertheless meeting life and death with peace of mind. It was necessary to hoist danger signals warning people against the Jews. And the church formulated its teaching about them all too hastily. The old painting in the church shows, in visual form, what the painter heard monks and priests preach about the Jews. Let us listen with him.

Once Israel was the chosen people, but that was long ago. The crown fell from its head when the Jews would not believe in Jesus, but murdered him in disbelief and hate. When they committed this terrible crime, God took the rights of the first-born away from Israel and gave them to the church. From that moment Judaism withered away; now it was a dead religion. The church was the new Israel. It inherited everything of value in the old Israel; its creative power and divine calling now belonged to the Christian Church.

But the Jews themselves were rejected. God punished and drove them out into exile all over the world. Really they ought to have been wiped out, to have disappeared from the face of the earth. But since they did exist, it must be because, under God's sentence, they served other people as an example of God's severity. Branded as Cain's descendants, stamped as deicides, with eternal guilt for the Crucifixion, they were forced to lead a hand-to-mouth existence of misery and fear. That was the moral of the story of the Wandering Jew who insulted Jesus on the way to Golgotha and as a punishment wandered ceaselessly from country to country and could never find rest.

The church was not content with stories and legends. The greatest theologian of the Middle Ages, St. Thomas Aquinas, was speaking officially on behalf of the Catholic Church when he laid it down that although the Jews ought not to be exterminated, yet they should be humbled for their sins and stubbornness. And the people of the church received instructions governing their attitude towards the Jews through Papal encyclicals, letters and conciliar decrees.

It was all those things that the great theologian Adolf Harnack had in mind when he caustically condemned the church's sin against Israel:

'The Gentile Christian church perpetrated an injustice unparalleled in history. It broke away from Judaism, but wrested everything away from it, too—its chosen status, the promises, the prophets. The daughter showed her mother the door, but only after robbing her of everything she possessed.'

We have seen what priests and monks said about the Jews. When such words are spoken over and over again, the common masses who hear them from the pulpit, at home and in the street, end up by wilfully setting fire to things. Evil instincts, fanaticism and fear combined with greed for the Jews' money and the promissory notes for Christian debts that lay hidden in their cupboards—it all ended in fire and slaughter. And this blood-red stripe that stains the history of the West has never been wholly whitened. To be sure, more moderate and polished speech prevails today. At Rome the Vatican Council discussed the problems, and the great majority of churchmen dissociated themselves from the accusations and prejudices. Yet the old ghosts have not been laid. A feeling of dislike still surrounds the Jew in Christian countries: he is different, he does not fit in. People have heard so many whispered rumours about him. The shadow of the spirit that inspired the artist to produce the painting on the church wall still falls on the Jews. The Jewish enigma stares the church in the face, misunderstood and accusing.

Israel and the church—two contrasts. The synagogue views the Christian belief in Jesus as heresy. The Jews could not and cannot accept an executed man as the Messiah and still less consider him to be God's son, for God is the first, therefore he has no father, and he is the last, consequently he has no son. God is one, holy, indivisible, alone. And the church lays down that Israel has long since had its day and now belongs to the past.

But superciliousness and conviction of one's superiority, no matter on which side they appear, are a sign of fossilisation, and no future can grow out of them. The man who listens only to himself, and is deaf to what his opponents say, is burying his head in the sand. That holds good for any place where Jew and Christian meet. The two religions sprang from the same source, and no matter how far apart their ways have carried them, they are for ever linked by fine threads, far more than they actually know, in a mysterious common destiny. They can never get rid of each other. This means, among many other things, that every Christian is two-thirds Jew, so close is the relationship. The church is impoverished if it comes to a stop with the Jews' denial of Jesus. For God hides secrets we do not understand and opens hidden ways to the people He never abandons.

We turn back to the little country church and stand in front of the painting of the two women once again. But now it is not only the synagogue that is blindfolded. The church also has a bandage over her eyes.

The time had come to produce another picture. It was painted by a Jew whose name was Martin Buber.

Martin Buber was for many years a personality in modern Judaism to whom both Jews and Christians listened. He was a professor at Frankfurt at the time when Nazi barbarity against the Jews was beginning to flourish. In spite of personal danger Buber stayed in the country as long as he possibly could. The Nazis did not dare to lay hands on him; instead they turned him into a sort of hostage by forcing him to be the representative of the German Jews in dealings with the authorities. Not until 1938 did Buber leave Germany and travel to Jerusalem to become professor at the Hebrew University. He died in 1965 at the age of eighty-seven. Throughout Buber's long life, one of the problems that preoccupied him was the schism between his own and the church's religion, and he uncovered brilliant truths and new horizons while studying it. While Buber was still living in Germany, he sketched the destiny of Israel and the church by citing an experience. His description of it is a counterpart to the painting in the church. I give it in Buber's own words:

'I live quite close to the city of Worms; I feel myself linked to it; my forefathers lived in Worms. Now and then I go into the city. The first thing I do in Worms is to visit the cathedral. There is a striking harmony between all its individual parts, a unity in which nothing detracts from perfection. Full of the joy inspired by beauty, I wander round the church, looking at it. Then I go further on, to the Jewish cemetery. It is full of crooked, cracked, misshapen and carelessly erected stones. I stand still and look up from the cemetery's confused mass of grey stones to the church's radiant harmony, and it is like looking up from Israel to the church. Down here, where I am, there is not a sign of beautiful shapes, only stones and the dust that is hidden beneath them. The dust is there, even if it is scattered and disappearing. The dust is something tangible; human beings who have become dust. It is there before my eyes. Not tangible like an actual place on this earth, but tangible in my memory, far back in the depths of history, as far back as Sinai.

'I have stood there; I have become one with the dust and through it with the patriarchs. It is the memory of the covenant with God, the pact that is held out to all Jews. The perfection of the Christian church cannot come between me and it; nothing is powerful enough to come between me and Israel's sacred history.

'I have stood there and experienced it all myself. These dead have met me; the dust, the ruins, the indescribable misery—they are all part of it together. But the covenant is not withdrawn from me. I am here on the earth, like one of these fallen stones. But the covenant is not taken from me. The cathedral is what it is. The stones are what they are. But nothing is taken from us.'*

In Buber's picture the two entities, the church and Israel, are confronting each other yet again, but not with facile foregone conclusions or judgments about one or the other. They simply meet, as their age-old destinies shaped them, the one in beauty and harmony, the other among tombs, in poverty. And even though the church is on high and Israel in the depths, they are on the same footing. There is eternity in both of them, invisible to the eye but founded on belief and given by the same God who has each of them in his thoughts.

Then comes the great question: Was it a tragedy that their ways parted or was it the intention of the All Highest that Judaism and Christianity should each go their own way for millennia?

That is the puzzle.

I know that merely posing such a question is provocative to people who are securely ensconced in safe, established dogmas. So I must console myself by agreeing with Tennyson when he says: 'There lives more faith in honest doubt, believe me, than in half the creeds.'

---

[1] Martin Buber: *Die Stunde und die Erkenntnis*, pp. 165-167.

The church teaches that Christianity's truth is absolute; it is the only way to heaven. It follows from this that Judaism is a false doctrine and its way does not lead to the goal, for from a purely logical point of view only one of two different philosophies can be right. Yet men forget that life is too many-sided to be laid bare with the help of electronic brains or tables of logarithms; all too often opposites are connected and inseparable. Unity between contrasts is one of life's strangely ironical replies to plain logic. There are truths so immense that they are only sensed in the form of a paradox.

Human beings are different. Some seek out narrow dangerous mountain paths with steep drops on either side. Others prefer the broad asphalted highway, where the truth is guaranteed and absolute and easy to handle. But it is the steep stony way that leads upwards and opens up panoramas that the others will never see. And even if no way leads so dizzily high that it reveals the vision of God's last secret about His ancient people and His also ancient, but younger church, it is worth venturing on the way, if only because it gives us the opportunity of seeing a great deal that the church has forgotten and needs to be reminded of again.

This book is written by a Christian who has become more firmly established in the traditional Christian faith by his researches into Jewish history and religion, but has simultaneously found new riches that are worth pointing out, because most Christians have never discovered the gold mine that is concealed in Judaism. For the Christian church has been so preoccupied that its elder sister, Judaism, has become an unknown factor, one of those white patches on the map where no Christian has set foot. In this respect Christianity is to an uncomfortable degree like an underdeveloped country. In church on Sunday we can hear glaring misapprehensions and stupid blunders being taught as infallible doctrine whenever the text concerns relations with Judaism. What is missing is the knowledge the church failed to give its servants.

Israel and the church. Nothing solves the puzzle, but we are going to set out to encompass it, as far as we can. The first thing to marvel at is the fact that the Jewish people exists, the second is the core of Jewish belief that Israel was chosen by God. Then we follow the way along which Israel wandered until it divided. Next we follow the two ways, the synagogue's and the church's, until finally we turn our gaze towards the far horizon, where the divided ways join up again.

B

'ZIMMERMANN, CAN YOU GIVE ME ONE single proof that God exists?'

Frederick the Great, King of Prussia, who was friendly with the sceptical Voltaire and shared his views, put this question to his physician-in-ordinary. Everyone knows the anecdote and the doctor's answer, which left the king speechless.

'The Jews, Your Majesty.'

Many others besides Frederick the Great were silenced when confronted with this people. Simply saying the word 'Jew' has always acted like a shock on cold scepticism and supercilious doubt. The Jewish people's survival sows doubts about the doubt.

In 1938, the year when bands of brown-uniformed S.A. men were sending German synagogues up in flames, Karl Barth published a volume of his systematic theology, in which he says:

'If anyone wants a proof of God, something visible and tangible that no one can deny and that is displayed for everyone to see, he must turn to the Jews.'

Karl Barth uses the expression 'tangible', something that *is*. In other words, a fact. And people profit by showing respect for hard facts. The existence of the Jewish people, living in the world today, is one of them.

But their existence is against all prevailing rules. According to the rules they should no longer exist.

Their saga covers the best part of four thousand years,

approximately two-thirds of the known history of mankind. A few small nomadic tribes became a people that was tossed about between mighty states—Egypt, Assyria, Babylon and Persia. The great nations clashed and destroyed one another in turn. There were times when Israel was on the verge of disappearing in the whirlpool caused by the collision of the giants. But it always bobbed up again above the foaming waves, though not to enjoy an untroubled existence. Hellas arose and stirred the ancient world as if with a magic wand; its spirit of beauty and harmony penetrated every nation— except the Jewish people. The Maccabees rose in revolt, the first war known to history for freedom of belief and thought, and cleansed Jerusalem of the contagion of Hellenism. And where is Hellas today? Its creative period lasted for 400 years; afterwards its spirit waned and its society deteriorated. The next act in the drama was Rome. Rome's legions crushed the Jewish state and the Jews were driven out all over the earth. Yet Rome perished and Israel lives. Dean Inge was right when he said that Israel had seen all its persecutors into the grave.

But their history did not end with the destruction of Jerusalem. During the next two thousand years the Jews were without a state, a government and an army. They lived scattered all over the world in small groups, despised, persecuted, rejected, exposed to attempts at conversion by Islam and the various Christian churches, and always on the verge of total annihilation. But they survived and preserved their national character and unity. The Jewish people's symbolism—a burning bush that is in flames but is not consumed—is an apt one.

What sort of secret is hidden in the Jewish people? Why does it, alone among all the others, continue to exist? It is like a tree that was torn up by the roots from its natural habitat and has never found a permanent home since. Yet against all common sense it thrives and blooms wherever it is replanted. There are other nations who were forced to pull up their tent poles and find new settlements. The migrations of peoples provide examples of this, and so do the waves of emigrants in more recent times, but all these peoples lost their special character as soon as their background changed. They simply vanished, merging with their new surroundings. Naturally they lent their strength to the others who imbibed their culture and were enriched thereby. Yet the wandering people remained apart. The Jews alone remained Jews; that is the unique feature of their destiny. History, which for the most part tells us of the absorption of minorities by majorities, offers this as a prime example of the opposite.

Old vanished cultures have left memorials of their existence in the form of material objects. We know and study them through the clay tablets, sites of houses, tombs, sculptures and coins unearthed by archaeologists. Jewish life in ancient times has left very few traces of that kind. There are some, but not many, that tell of battles lost or won, and fallen greatness. The most important heritage that the ancient Jews left posterity does not exist in stone and bronze, but lives in thoughts, visions and ideas. The paradoxical thing is that the peoples over whom proud moments and ruins stand as memorials perished and disappeared. The Jews bequeathed their ideas and they still live.

Byron has a moving couplet about Jewish destiny:

'The wild dove has her nest, the fox his cave,
Mankind their country—Israel but the grave.'

Byron is right, if he is thinking of the age-old tragedy with its sorrow and tears, but he does not say that this is only one side of the picture. The other says that Israel still lives, above countless graves that hide the victims of intolerance and hate. Like a sphinx that is silent behind its mysterious smile, the unanswered question remains: Why does the Jewish people exist today and remain Jewish?

Our century has seen two gifted and audacious historians develop systems that aim at nothing less than incorporating the history of mankind from the very beginnings of time. Both of them are not afraid of asserting that they know the answers to questions that leave the rest of us baffled. I mean

Oswald Spengler and Arnold Toynbee. The former attracted attention with his pessimistic prophecy about the imminent decline of the West; the latter has been in the news since he began to publish his massive *Study of History*.

Both assert that history is not a fortuitous process, a series of random events, but a stream in which one event develops from another. Cultures are like living beings. They are conceived, born and grow up through childhood, youth and middle age, then they finally grow old and die. This far Spengler and Toynbee keep company, but afterwards their ways part.

For Oswald Spengler everything living is doomed to die. He sees every new culture as a bloom that buds in spring, ripens in summer, bears fruit in autumn and dies when winter sets in. He calls his system cyclical, i.e. wheel-shaped. In it a culture rolls up like a wheel from bottom to top and then rolls down and disappears. But here the Jewish destiny rises in protest. True enough, the Jews began their history with a spring, heralded by a new religion that was the core of their culture. Summer and autumn followed with flowers and fruit, but winter and death never overtook them. It is as if their development came to a stop between autumn and winter. Obviously Spengler ought to explain why the Jews deviate from his pattern like this. But we look for an explanation in vain; Spengler ignores the Jews. In his work we only find what we already know, that the Jews are the unexplained exception.

But what about Arnold Toynbee? He calls his a linear system. According to it no culture need die; each one holds its destiny in its own hands. If a culture possesses the will to live, it can, as if following a straight line, develop eternally from lower to higher forms. Toynbee's key words are: Challenge—Response. As long as a culture responds to the challenges it meets, and overcomes them, it lives and develops. But if it is passive, it comes to a halt, as the Eskimos and Hottentots did, because they never harnessed themselves to the chariot of history. A stagnant culture of this kind ends up as a fossil, something that lived once, but died so long ago that today it is a petrifaction.

The Jews seem to fit this pattern like a glove. They did in fact respond to one challenge after another. They left Egypt and struggled through the wilderness, they conquered the promised land, the Maccabees rose in rebellion, to cite but a few examples. And the Jews still live today—the straight line has never been broken. So far so good. However, we are left with the essence of the question, which Toynbee never answers. Where does he find the source of the Jews' vitality; who gave them the ardent will to defy destiny over and over again? For that is where the problem lies. Yet not only is Toynbee silent, but also, incredible as it may sound, he removes Judaism from his system and reduces it to the state of a fossil. In other words, he puts the Jews on a par with the Hottentots and Eskimos. This calls for an explanation.

The fact is that Toynbee is as much a prophet as a historian. The difference between the scholar and the prophet is that the former bows to the facts he meets and forms his theory according to them, whereas the prophet is tempted to do violence to facts in order to bring them into line with his dogmas. Toynbee's system is vulnerable to criticism of this kind. And one of the weak points in his otherwise impressive work is his treatment of the enigma of Judaism. It has given rise to a flood of objections.

Toynbee's dogma is that evolution aspires to a universal state with an equally universal religion, an orchestra in which every religion plays its own instrument. But there is no place in it for Judaism, because it has always refused to be absorbed. Therefore Toynbee stamps it as a fossil. It died when the Jews refused to recognise Jesus as the Messiah and Son of God.

But here the dogmatist meets one of the facts that ought to bowl his theory over. In our own time Judaism has revealed such vitality that it has won back its lost country, created a new Jewish state and defended it in victorious wars. How can a fossil that died 1,900 years ago be the author of such achievements? The fact that Toynbee brushes aside this objection by retorting that Israel was born in sin because it captured an Arab country and put its inhabitants to flight is outside the scope of this chapter, but I mention it because it further characterises this great historian as a dogmatist the moment one of his pet theories enters the danger zone. And since our main concern is seeking an answer to the riddle of Judaism, we must leave Toynbee without having found it.

Things go no better for us if we seek the answer within the framework of Marxism's materialist concept of history. Is the Jews' survival really supposed to be the result of the material conditions under which the people lived? Was it the state of the soil and methods of cultivation, economic relations with neighbouring countries or fluctuations in the price of figs and olives that created monotheism, the faith in the one almighty God? Did economic conditions under Omri and Josiah inspire the prophets with their visions?

We must not treat such considerations too lightly. No one should minimise the influence of material factors on spiritual development and strength. Shortage of rain, navigable channels on the sea, curves showing the increase in population, the merchants' caravan routes—everything in nature and the world of men, including the spirit's highest flights, is interwoven and together creates the variegated mosaic we call life. And yet the achievement of a little people like the Jews—dispersed, despised, persecuted—in managing to steer a course through the millennia of history and remain the same, is so unparalleled that these explanations are inadequate. The stars are still too high for us to be able to put them under a magnifying glass.

So we had better listen to those who say that antisemitism provides an explanation. It did drive the Jews into isolation and force them to mobilise their powers of resistance to the utmost. It has been vividly expressed by saying that the Jewish people is eternal, not because it was allowed to live, but because men did not allow it to live. Precisely because it had to give more than life, it won life.

Here we come to one aspect of the problem that touches on Toynbee's Challenge-Response and is of considerable importance. Evil times are often good in the sense that they arouse and steel the will to survive. Everyone knows that good times lull people into a false sense of security. The sentries fall asleep if they think that the enemy is far away. The most dangerous crisis Judaism went through began when it found itself surrounded by tolerance and a moderate amount of good will. But for centuries the Jews learnt from bitter experience. They were exiled and defenceless against the brutality and fanaticism and greed that were always on their trail. Yet nature teaches the weak to protect themselves and develop the qualities they need. The Jews learnt to bow when the storm raged; they learnt coolness and ingenuity. The Jews became more worldly-wise than their enemies.

A great many things in the Jews' long history have their explanation in considerations such as these. But they do not provide the whole answer. This complex, made up of so many varied, twisted threads, looks more entangled the more one ponders over the problem. In every reckoning a fraction is left that cannot be reduced. Let us use a word that leads our thoughts to higher spheres—mystery. Thought knocks in vain at the door to the mystery. It is opened only from within, and then not more than half way—by the hand of the All Highest alone.

It is as if God holds His ancient chosen people in reserve for a plan we half-blind human beings cannot glimpse and which the Almighty guards as His secret. God gave us His revelation in Holy Writ, but it does not stop with those written words. Jewish history extends beyond both the Old and the New Testaments. Where the Bible stops, it continues and aspires to the end; it points to the Messiah.

A gleam from above shines through the gap in the closed door. God reveals one side of His nature, His faithfulness. Over Jewish history stands a *semper fidelis* (always faithful).

Not Israel's fidelity, but God's. He does not go back on His promise, the promise made to Israel when He chose them as His own 'peculiar people'.

No one gets any closer. When we men in the world of mortal clay try to interpret the mystery of eternity, we grope our way forward in darkness and have to solve one riddle by asking another, as it were. We are faced with God's choice of Israel.

3 / THE CHOSEN

ATTA VECHARTANU MIKOL HA'AMIM. THESE are the words of a Hebrew prayer that has been recited from the festival prayer-book on the great Jewish holy-days for centuries: 'Thou hast chosen us from all peoples.' And the prayer continues:

'Thou hast loved us and taken pleasure in us, and hast exalted us above all tongues; and thou hast sanctified us by thy commandments, and brought us near unto thy service, O our King, and hast called us by Thy great and holy name.'

The prayer is one of many examples of Israel's happy knowledge that God has created a unique bond between Himself and His people. Near the end of all synagogue services the congregation recites a prayer which is so old that it can be traced back to the third century and which is called after its first word, *Alenu* (It is our duty). *Alenu* proclaims God's greatness and unity in such forthright words that the medieval church considered it an attack on its doctrine of the Trinity and forbade it. *Alenu* has been aptly called the Marseillaise of the Jewish genius. It, too, rings with Israel's consciousness of its election:

'It is our duty to praise the Lord of all things, to ascribe greatness to Him who formed the world in the beginning. Since He hath not made us like the nations of other lands, and hath not placed us like other families of the earth; since He hath not assigned unto us a portion as unto them, nor a lot as unto all their multitude.'

Here we stand by the rock on which Judaism was erected. These prayers are not merely pious words. There is destiny in them. The first time an outsider hears them, they jar on his ears with their ring of arrogance and chauvinism. But Judaism must never be judged by first impressions. It is a world in itself; it was born in a past so remote that it is lost in the mists of time and it has grown up over thousands of years. Its Hebraic liturgical language comes from a period that lies much further back than the Greek and Latin of the Orthodox and Roman Churches; its liturgical music was old when the Latins learnt the Gregorian chant. And its consciousness of election is the bond which keeps the people so firmly linked to vanished generations that it literally makes the Jew of today a contemporary of Abraham. Knowledge to be proud of that raises the Jew above adversity and envy, but far more it is a reminder of an eternal responsibility. It is this tension between God's gift and His demands that we meet wherever we look for information in Judaism and that through changing ages created its immutable image.

The doctrine of election has solid basis in the Bible. We read in Deuteronomy 14 : 2 :

'For thou art an holy people unto the Lord thy God, and the Lord hath chosen thee to be a peculiar people unto Himself, above all the nations that are upon the earth.'

Every Bible reader can find many passages that express the same idea. Naturally learned and pious rabbis have pondered over this and developed the doctrine in many details. Scattered through the books of the Talmud we find quotations of their discussions, a motley mixture of wise words and droll parables. We leaf through them and find a blend of sublime and trivial material. Before the world was created, God knew that He would choose His Israel. Eternal Israel, as well as the Torah and the Messiah's name, already existed then; they exist today and will do so for ever. God made the covenant, first with Abraham, for whom circumcision was the sign, then with the whole people at Sinai, when the Torah was given. However, it concerned not only the generation of Israel that was gathered at Sinai, but all generations to come. Here is one of the Talmud's legends: When God called Moses up to Sinai, there were seventy nations in the world, and God proclaimed His Torah in all their seventy languages. From distant lands came scribes who took down the Torah, each in his own language, and took it home with them. But all the other nations rejected it and refused to obey it. The last people that was asked was Israel. It said yes and swore obedience, and that is why God chose it.

In other words, Israel deserved to become the chosen people. We meet the same idea in the lines:

> How odd
> of God
> to choose
> the Jews,

and Hilaire Belloc's answer:

> It was not odd,
> The Jews chose God.[1]

But Judaism is not as superficial as legend and poetry would have us believe. There is some truth in saying that a covenant is mutual; both parties make an undertaking. God chooses the people and they promise obedience. But most rabbis have always been aware that at bottom it was God who acted; the covenant was an arrangement by Him alone. It was not based on any merit of Israel's, but on His love. And to love is to choose. The Bible realises this, too:

'The Lord did not set His love upon you, nor choose you, because ye were more in number than any people; for ye were the fewest of all people:

'But because the Lord loved you, . . .'

The choice applies to Israel. In other words, the people,

---

[1] The author of the first four lines is William Norman Ewer, born 1885. The last two are generally supposed to have been written by the witty, paradox-loving Gilbert Keith Chesterton. However, it was his friend Hilaire Belloc who actually wrote them. The two friends were not always so kindly disposed towards the Jews. We can see this from the proposed epitaph, written with genuine Jewish wit: Here lies Gilbert Chesterton—who to Heaven would have gone—if he had not heard the news—that the place is run by Jews!

knesset Israel (the congregation of Israel). It is typically Jewish that the whole precedes the individual. Here we come to
one of the distinctions between the synagogue and the church.
In Christianity God's choice concerns the individual; in
Judaism a person is chosen because he is one of the chosen
people. God deals with Israel and through it with the individual Jew. If the individual and the collective are considered as opposites, the church emphasises the former, the
synagogue the latter. For the concept of the people in Judaism has a position that is foreign to the rest of us. The Jew
of today is a microscopic fragment of the Jewish people,
which is much vaster than our conception of it, for it includes
not only the generation that is living now, but also all dead
and future, still unborn generations. Israel is like a living
organism, at one and the same time age-old and new and
young, yet fundamentally always the same. An abyss yawns
between the farmer of King Solomon's time who tended his
fig trees in one of Judaea's valleys and the coldly calculating
stress-ridden banker in New York's Wall Street. But they
are limbs of the same body; an eternal bond links them together. The bond is God's choice of Israel.

At first glance Israel's election looks like privilege. But
its alpha and omega is responsibility, God's demand. And
just look what it has cost the people who shouldered the
burden! 'Israel is like an olive,' we read in the Talmud,
'which only yields its precious oil when it is pressed and
squeezed. It was Israel's destiny to experience oppression and
suffering in order to give others its wisdom.' And the Spanish
twelfth-century poet-philosopher, Yehuda Halevi, expresses
Israel's mission in another image:

'God's wise and secret plan for us can be compared to
the seed that falls in the field. It disappears, disintegrates and
looks like earth and water, without apparently leaving a trace.
But in reality it is the seed that changes earth and water and
compels the elements according to its nature, not theirs, and
raises them, so that it and they together become a tree with
leaves and fruit.'

No, the choice does not narrow Israel's horizon, for its message is universal, as God is. 'Have we all not one father? hath not one God created us?' says the prophet Malachi, whose book is the last in the Hebrew Bible.

Ancient Greece created a people of philosophers and artists; the foundations of the law and statesmanship of later times were laid in ancient Rome. These two bequeathed a heritage that still shapes western culture. But it is Israel's religious genius that completes the triad in the world of to-day and gives it depth and warmth. Judaism gives its evidence of God's reality and unity, which are without compare.

It is thoughts like these that are set in motion by the idea of Israel's election. But we never get beyond the perimeter. The ultimate secret constantly hides its face behind the closed door; we never grasp the riddle and the mystery behind God's choice of Israel. The element of eternity defies both thoughts and words. We only guess that a God who is high above and infinitely remote from our comprehension, chose Israel as His peculiar people for a reason He alone knows.

But we can follow the visible side of the choice in Israel's life, as it forcibly fits the eternal people into God's plan, which, in the fulness of time, forced God's other people into the Christian church.

4 / EXILE

PALESTINE CAME INTO EXISTENCE THROUGH an earthquake. Geology tells of a terrestrial catastrophe; the globe split and an enormous rift opened from Syria in the north down through what is the Jordan valley today, the Gulf of Aqaba, the Red Sea and further on right down to the great African lakes. No imagination can possibly depict the details of this drama, but Palestine was created as a result of it. It is symbolic that an earthquake was the reason for this country's coming into being. For as long as people can remember, Palestine has stood under the sign of an earthquake, politically speaking.

It could not be otherwise. Palestine is a bridge, a narrow strip of land with the sea on one side and the desert on the other. Its destiny decreed that this narrow bridge was the only practicable route that joined two continents, Africa and Asia, and in olden times two of the world's oldest cultures, together. The route from Egypt by way of Palestine to the valley of the Euphrates is one of the oldest on earth. Along it travelled not only peaceful caravans with prosperity and progress in their train, but also the armies of the great powers. Palestine became the plaything of powers that were stronger than she was. The red thread of catastrophe that has entwined the fabric of Jewish history ever since was being woven even then.

One of the catastrophes was total—not only did it mean the downfall of a state, but the majority of the Jewish people disappeared in it too. In the seventh century B.C. Assyria's war machine disrupted and terrorised the Middle East; there was no army or fortress able to halt its bloody but triumphant progress. Terror-stricken, the Kingdom of Judah avoided becoming embroiled and kept its neutrality, but the Northern Kingdom dared to resist. The result was defeat, devastation, deportation. Most of the people were carried off and disappeared in the Orient's sea of races; no one knows what became of the exiles.

One hundred and thirty-six years after the downfall of Samaria, in 586 B.C., came the turn of the Kingdom of Judah. Now the world power was called Babylon and its king Nebuchadnezzar. He put down all resistance in two bloody campaigns. Jerusalem defended itself for more than a year. But even its mighty town walls crumbled and fell in ruins under the onslaught of the besiegers' battering-rams, and the city was conquered. Nebuchadnezzar razed Jerusalem to the ground and deported the flower of the people to Babylon. King Zedekiah was captured while fleeing. In the Babylonian headquarters at Kadesh, by the River Orontes, he suffered the fate reserved for a rebellious vassal. In chains, he saw his sons murdered, then his eyes were put out.

Nearly a third of Judah's inhabitants were killed during the war. Of the survivors every 'man of might' and his family were taken away into captivity. Only the impoverished country dwellers were allowed to stay behind.

When Nebuchadnezzar's name is remembered today it is solely because of this event. Without knowing or wanting it, he set in motion a chain reaction that acquired significance for the whole of mankind. It was during the captivity in Babylon that the Jewish people found itself, so that it could survive the catastrophes that were to shake it for thousands of years. Here a development germinated that later put forth flowers. Human culture would have been different if it had not been for the exiled people by the rivers of Babylon.

In the view of the ancients, a people's political and

military defeat was evidence of their gods' inferiority. As an inflexible rule the defeated rejected their old gods and took over, and bowed down to the gods of the victors. It is unique in history that the captives from Jerusalem went directly against this tendency. The meaning of the prophets' teaching dawned on them. They realised that it was not God who had failed them. No, *they* had failed Him with their sins and apostasy, and now they were receiving their punishment. For God was the one, the almighty; in His hand the victors were merely tools for carrying out His plans. Therefore they dared to believe that their history had not petered out and ended with the catastrophe. There was a future for them if they were obedient to God's will.

Otherwise, the temptation to become assimilated, with the gradual disappearance of national consciousness, must have been obvious in Babylon. Its brilliant, cosmopolitan culture fascinated the defeated, cowed Jerusalemites. The capital was a world city teeming with people of every country, race and language. Its walls covered more than fifty miles; they were so wide that four chariots could drive side by side on them. Jerusalem had had its one temple, but here there were fifty-five great temples, sumptuously decorated with gold and jewels, where only the most important gods were worshipped, in addition to countless small ones. In the midst of the splendour towered the colossal statue of the god Marduk, and as far as the eye could see there were soaring towers and hanging gardens. There were plenty of others, apart from the provincials from a primitive remote country, who stopped short to gape at the capital's breathtaking magnificence.

Babylon, as a general rule, treated conquered peoples leniently.

Deportation was not a punitive measure but a political move. Palestine was a strategic centre; it was the way to the arch-enemy, Egypt, and even more important it was the latter's invasion route to Babylon. It might be dangerous if the leading men of Palestine took it into their heads to flirt

c

with the Pharaohs. So they were taken away. The common ignorant men who were left behind plotting and planning were not regarded as dangerous.

Nebuchadnezzar also counted on enterprising people among his new subjects making a useful contribution to the industrial life of the empire. Consequently he settled them in Mesopotamia's richest regions, around the town of Nippur by the River Chedar, where they planted gardens and tilled the soil, while others in the towns were bankers and businessmen. We have a glimpse of the details of this commercial life from the discovery of 700 clay tablets inscribed with the accounts of a business firm in Nippur. The Israelites bowed to destiny in these conditions that were forced on them; they followed the prophet Jeremiah's injunction to seek the peace of the city the Lord had led them to, for 'in the peace thereof shall ye have peace'.

If carried out literally, such a line of action would have led directly to assimilation. And, of course, elements of Babylonian culture did become part of Israelite life. In the course of time Babylonian names, details of the calendar and customs were adopted. But this only disturbed the surface. Evidence of this is the immortal psalm about home-sickness, which was written in exile:

'By the rivers of Babylon, there we sat down, yea, we wept, when we remembered Zion . . . If I forget thee, O Jerusalem, let my right hand forget her cunning.'

Babylon could tempt and excite; it seemed to possess all the loveliness of the earth. Nevertheless, the Israelites felt superior. Each one of them, even the lowliest, was of noble birth; they were all descended from Abraham, Isaac and Jacob. The patriarch's covenant with the Almighty bound them too; they could never renounce so great a heritage of promise and obligation. And soon their spiritual leaders discovered a form of religion that replaced what they had lost and kept them assembled in the covenant with all the former greatness.

It had seemed the obvious thing to build a temple and

continue the traditional sacrificial services. But no, Jerusalem, the holy city, remained bright in their memories; only there could the Lord be worshipped as He had been by their fathers. Faced with that fact, all ideas of making a copy faded. Moreover, they could not procure ritually clean offerings of animals and crops that were reared or grown on their home ground. Instead they met without temple and sacrifices to pray and listen to readings and interpretations of the holy scriptures. This took place on the Sabbath, at new moon and on the big holidays. Here something new germinated. The foundations of the synagogue were laid—the way of life which was to preserve Judaism intact throughout the exile and which provided the inspiration for Christian services.

The scriptures that were read at the services were a heritage from home brought with them to Babylon. We do not know what they looked like, but they were probably written on tablets or vellum, as was the custom of ancient peoples. These rarities were precious to those who possessed them. Often such a text was the only object saved from a burning house on the day when Babylon's soldiery went plundering. Some were bloodstained, because the owner had defended it against a flashing sword-stroke with his body. But many texts were not yet written down. They had lived from mouth to mouth: songs, psalms, legends, rituals, laws, prophecies and historical annals.

When history stands still, the memory of the past awakes. The man who stands in the midst of the stream of events does not write about them, for he is fully occupied by the moment. Most men only reach for the pen when peace has descended on their minds. During the long period of waiting in Babylon, the Israelites steeped themselves in their literary treasure. Books took on new life; a gleam of vanished greatness shone around them. So they were read and studied, collected and commented on over and over again. Here Israel became the bookish people it has been ever since. Much of the Hebrew Bible was collected into its canon at Babylon.

New holy scriptures came into being at Babylon. Ezekiel

consoled his people and prophesied God's judgment on the heathens. And he promised a new future for Israel. In visions burning so intensely that they indicate a mind that was on the verge of a breakdown, he painted pictures of the chariot of fire, later an inexhaustible source for mystics, and proclaimed the Lord's will to bring dry bones to life, 'and I will . . . bring you into the land of Israel'. But Ezekiel was not only a father of mysticism. He was the son of a priest and a priest himself. The fiery visions belong to his youth. With the maturity of age the priest's ability to prepare and organise awakened. In his prophetic visions of life in the home country, the temple and the priests are the centre, with the holy Torah as a guide. Here we have a theocracy, God's dominion, or more accurately a state that is run by the priesthood. In the Jewish tradition Ezekiel is considered as one of the major prophets. His ideas had far-reaching effects, indeed the essence of them still stamps the Jewish philosophy of life. The Spanish writer Unamuno has said of another Jew, Baruch Spinoza, that he suffered from 'god's-ache'. As other people can be tormented by tooth-ache or ear-ache, this god's-ache never left Spinoza in peace. It can be said of Ezekiel that he was 'intoxicated with God'.

In Babylon the Israelites felt themselves in the same situation as their fathers under Moses in the wilderness on their wandering towards the promised land. It was here the Lord revealed His Torah. And now in Babylon He gave them what they needed to preserve their distinctive character—instructions to individual and community regulating life according to His will. As a result the men who studied the Torah acquired a special status. The priests were no longer confined to temple services; now they had the time and energy to study the Torah and instruct the people in it. These priests are often spoken of disparagingly in comparison with the prophets. True enough, they seldom produced outstanding personalities. But they had their natural place in a development that began to prepare the way in Babylon for the ideal image of the people as holy and the democratisation of the prophets' creed, which became a national heritage in Israel.

Nebuchadnezzar lived a long time; he reigned for forty years. He had ruled his empire autocratically and been feared by his neighbours. His death set the usual oriental schemings in motion: intrigues, palace revolutions and assassinations. His son was murdered; only a couple of weak kings succeeded him.

But a new star rose above the horizon. With fantastic speed the youthful Cyrus established a new empire—the Persian empire. Cyrus was the greatest statesman and general of his age. He went from victory to victory; his rule extended all the way to the Aegean Sea. Asia Minor was conquered and rumour had it that he was arming for a campaign against Babylon itself.

The Middle East's rulers and nations followed the new ruler's exploits with mixed feelings. Kings began to tremble; the conquered took hope.

None listened so anxiously for news from the theatres of war as the deported Israelites. They began to hold up their heads again. For decade after decade they had waited for something to happen. Dreamers and seers had foretold divine intervention. Realists counted on something more tangible. But they had one feeling in common. This state of affairs could not go on; the exile must come to an end. Rumour ran ahead of the Persian army and told of Cyrus's magnanimity, his tolerance of other people's religions. In truth, here gleamed the hope of return home.

An echo of expectation comes back to us from the conclusion of the Book of Isaiah 40-66, whose author we do not know. (He is called Deutero-Isaiah or the second Isaiah.) He, the loftiest spirit among all the prophets, went out into the markets and bazaars and proclaimed his joyful message:

'Comfort ye, comfort ye my people, saith your God.

'Speak ye comfortably to Jerusalem, and cry unto her that her warfare is accomplished, that her iniquity is pardoned.'

The day of liberation was at hand:

'Go ye forth of Babylon, flee ye from the Chaldeans . . .
utter it even to the end of the earth; say ye, The Lord hath
redeemed his servant Jacob.'

The instrument of liberation was Cyrus, the heathen,
who, without knowing the true God, had to carry out His
will. The Almighty caused Babylon to fall in order to restore
Judah. And the prophet proclaims in soaring visions that
God is the God of the whole world, the only one. Israel is his
servant, in the 53rd chapter, the Suffering Servant of the
Lord; through his suffering the peoples are redeemed of their
sins. Here the prophet bridges the gulf between nationalism
and universalism; Israel is Israel, but it serves mankind.

The expectation was fulfilled. The drama of Babylon's
fall was enacted; the Persian army's assault proved irresistible.
After Babylon's army had lost the first great battle, people
hailed the conqueror as the new sovereign. The defeated
powerless king was deposed and Cyrus made his entry into
the captured capital. He treated the vanquished with clem-
ency and respected their gods. So much we know from Babylonian sources, which describe the change of power factually
and dryly. But tradition and legend also dwell on the event
and embellish it with vivid details. Perhaps they only
conceal confused memories, unacceptable to historical
research, but they still belong to the traditional picture of
this turning point in both the old world's and Israel's
history.

We find the Biblical account of the event in the Book of
Daniel. In it the last king of Babylon is called Belshazzar. At
a nocturnal feast the king and his guests drink from golden
beakers that had been stolen from the temple in Jerusalem.
A mysterious hand appears and writes unintelligible words
on the wall. The king has an uneasy foreboding and calls for
his soothsayers and astrologers, but they are unable to interpret the writing. Only the Israelite sage Daniel can do so.
He reads the words 'Mene, mene, tekel, upharsin' and trans-
lates them, 'Numbered, numbered, weighed and found want-

ing, thy kingdom is divided'. On the same night the Persians kill the king. Both the chronology and the people's names are confused, but in its dreamlike poetic form the biblical legend is evidence of the popular conviction that Babylon's fall was connected with the profanation of the temple in Jerusalem. We hear an echo of the prophet's words about the ruler of the world as a tool in the Lord's hand.

/

Cyrus made his entry into Babylon and proclaimed himself as liberator, not conqueror. And his first edicts showed that there was substance behind his words. He turned the fallen dynasty's national and religious policy upside down. It had accumulated the idols and holy symbols of conquered countries, and here Cyrus, like so many kings after him, came up against a Jewish problem. For one of the peoples that had been uprooted and carried off into exile along with the temple's precious treasure was made up of the inhabitants of Jerusalem. Cyrus himself believed in a single god; he was bound to look sympathetically on Israel with its even stricter monotheism.

But there was cold political calculation behind Cyrus's decision to allow Judah's people to return to their home country and rebuild the temple. He wanted to see his newly won frontier province successfully reconstructed and its grateful people in such a position that he could rely on them as sentinels against Egypt.

In his first year as king of Babylon Cyrus issued from his summer residence as Ecbatan, the modern Hamadan, the manifesto that permitted Judah's people to return and rebuild the temple, and said that the sacred silver and gold vessels that Nebuchadnezzar carried off should be given back and restored to their rightful place in the newly-built temple. Fragments of the manifesto can be read in two different places in the Book of Ezra.

The pious author of the book writes that 'all them whose spirit God had raised' prepared for the journey. In other words, he realised that something special was required to take the great decision to return home. For it was true that it meant facing an uncertain future. Even then only those who dared to venture everything became Zionists; those who were not content to be contributors, but gave themselves. During the half century the people had lived in Babylon, there were many who had established themselves and were now living well. It is by no means easy to make a break with a comfortable existence and travel to a place where you know that a hard and laborious future awaits you.

The majority remained in Babylon; and other areas of the Persian Empire. In Iran today, under the benevolent rule of the Shah, large numbers of Jews live in freedom. However, following the outbreak of Israeli-Arab hostilities, most Jews left Iraq, formerly Mesopotamia, where their ancestors had remained after the overthrow of Babylon. While the majority of Iraqi Jewry were conveyed to the State of Israel, through operation Ali Baba, a diminutive Jewish community is still in being in Iraq today.

We know the numbers of Judah's people who took the risk and returned home. In the Book of Ezra the figure is given as 42,360, besides servants and handmaids; altogether about 50,000 people, quite a considerable band. Those who remained behind saw to the finances and provisions. The joyfulness of those who went home was expressed in Psalm 126:

'When the Lord turned again the captivity of Zion, we were like them that dream.

'Then was our mouth filled with laughter, and our tongue with singing . . .'

When a new bridge is finished, it is subjected to the load test. The engineers put on it many times the weight they estimate the bridge will have to bear and follow its oscillations closely. Not until the check is satisfactory is the bridge opened to traffic. The fifty years of captivity Judah's people lived through was such a load test. A century and a half previously the people of the Northern Kingdom were tested in the same way—the so-called Ten Lost Tribes. They did not pass the test. The bridge collapsed, and the people disappeared in the Assyrian tidal wave.

But Judah's people *did* pass it. They had proved their will to live and found the way of life they were to develop in. Israel's youth had come to an end; its manhood was beginning.

5 / EZRA

TODAY CAR OR BUS SPEEDS THE TRAVELLER through the vast deserts that separate the valley of the Euphrates containing Babylon's ruins from modern Palestine. But even now the journey seems long. A monotonous flat desert landscape extends from horizon to horizon, interrupted but rarely by inhabited settlements, where the desert changes into semi-desert, with stunted dry vegetation. And while the car rushes on at eighty miles an hour, his thoughts fly back one and a half thousand years to the time when the liberated people struggled on their homeward way, the same way along which their ancestor Abraham in still remoter times had wandered at the Lord's command to find the land that was given to him and his seed.

The caravans trailed slowly on. Camels and herds of cattle set the tempo; the day's march was short before camp was pitched for the night. In the sparsely populated regions they met old enemies, Aramaeans and Ammonites, but they had safe conducts to show and Persian soldiers to escort them. At last, after four months' wandering, they reached the ford over the Jordan and set foot on their ancient land. As returning Jews do to this day, they fell on their knees and kissed the soil. They were home again.

Babylon's new ruler sent them away in style. The expedition had distinguished leaders. Two princes of royal descent, both of David's house, Sheshbazzar and Zerubbabel, were entrusted with the command by Cyrus. By their side was the high priest, Jeshua, who was descended from King

Solomon's first high priest, Zadok. They took the temple treasure with them and a letter of royal support for the reconstruction of the temple.

As soon as they glimpsed the familiar outline of Judaea's mountains in the distance above the horizon, their joy was great. But when they made their entry and saw things at close quarters, their enthusiasm flagged. The spectacle was not encouraging. Jerusalem was deserted; grass and weeds grew high in empty streets and among ruins, devastated houses, blackened beams and crumbling stones. Those who had remained behind were poverty-stricken, scattered and few in number; they lived in the country towns which clung to the mountain sides or lay hidden in valleys. The country was small; it measured only thirty miles from north to south. The former vassals, Edomites, Ammonites and Philistines, watched with sour looks. They had dreamt of taking possession of the deserted country and had already infiltrated on all sides. But now the country was inhabited by its rightful owners, and under Persian protection into the bargain.

The biggest task was to rebuild the temple. A religious revival had swept the people; they looked on their homecoming as a gift from the Lord. The temple was to be a symbol of His presence and help. When the first autumn month of Tishri, the New Year, came, the temple ruins were cleared and the altar for burnt offerings was rebuilt. Preparations for building went on; contracts for dressed stone and cedar trees were placed. One year after the homecoming, in the spring month of Iyar, the foundation-stone was laid. From far and near the people assembled, but weeping was heard in the midst of song and jubilation. The old ones, who remembered Solomon's temple in all its glory, could not restrain their tears when they discovered how modestly the new temple was planned.

But it is one thing to begin, another to carry the work to its conclusion, especially if unexpected obstacles crop up, as they did in Jerusalem.

First from the north. The Samaritans lived in the ancient

Northern Kingdom. They were a mixed race, remnants of the original inhabitants and heathen colonists fused together. The Israelite creed and heathen elements were interwoven in their everyday life and customs. But when the Samaritans heard of their kinsmen's homecoming, memories of the past awoke and they asked Zerubbabel if they could share in the rebuilding of the temple. The answer was a rebuff. Zerubbabel was afraid of exposing his people's purity and religion to contagion. His brusque snub had far-reaching consequences. The Samaritans retaliated by attacking; they intrigued with the Persian court and created serious difficulties for Jerusalem.

Even more obstacles piled up. Cyrus's successor, Cambyses, went to war against Egypt. Palestine became a battlefield again, with foreign troops who moved backwards and forwards through the country. After the war came revolt and disintegration in Persia; drought and crop failure set in and brought poverty and distress. It took Jerusalem a long time to rise from the ruins. Depression weighed the people down; passivity and resignation set their mark on the homecomers. The temple lay there like a skeleton.

'You looked for much, and, lo, it came to little; and when ye brought it home, I did blow upon it. Why? saith the Lord of hosts. Because of mine house that is waste, and ye run every man unto his own house.

'Therefore the heaven over you is stayed from dew, and the earth is stayed from her fruit.'

A prophet raised his voice in the streets of Jerusalem and people listened enthralled to strains they had heard their fathers talk about. The prophet Haggai spoke now in simple, easily intelligible words. He promised that the new temple's fame would outshine the old. A great future awaited Zerubbabel and the people.

Zechariah, the other prophet of the age, made even loftier promises. He painted in visions that surpass Ezekiel's in beauty, and foretold that foreign nations would seek out Jerusalem and ask the Lord for mercy. Some of his words have become winged and are always remembered. He it was who warned against despising 'the day of small things', and one of Judaism's mottoes was his work: 'Not by might, nor by power, but by my spirit,' saith the Lord of hosts.

The prophets' judgments and promises finally roused the people. Building was resumed and the temple completed. It was consecrated at Passover with great pomp and ceremony. Even though it was smaller and far less brilliantly decorated than Solomon's temple, it was nevertheless a temple and abode for the All Highest. The consecration took place in 516 B.C., exactly seventy years after the destruction of the first temple. So Jewish tradition reckons that the Babylonian captivity lasted those seventy years.

A milestone in Israel's history had been passed. And with it the curtain goes down. History is silent about the many years that followed. The great promises were not fulfilled. Judaea remained a rather small and unimportant country in the mighty Persian empire, which stretched from India to Ethiopia and the deserts of Libya. It occupied no more space than a postage stamp. It was during these years that the name 'Jews' became the designation for the people of Judaea and their kinsmen in all countries. They had called themselves the children of Judah or Benjamin, but their enemies used the word 'Jews' contemptuously. It is not the only time that a nickname became a general designation. The word 'Christian' underwent the same development.

For more than half a century after the reconstruction of the temple, Judaea remained in darkness. The broken threads were not joined again until one of Judaism's brilliant figures took the stage. His name was Ezra.

'For, lo, the winter is past, the rain is over and gone.

'The flowers appear on the earth; the time of the singing of the birds is come . . .'

With these verses the poet of the Song of Solomon greets the advent of spring in Judaea's valleys. The words have become classical; they echo in the mind every year when we experience life's victory over the dead season of winter with renewed amazement. But in Judaism the spring song is also used about Ezra and his deeds. With him a new age burst forth, with blossom and fruit. He stands high in popular tradition, which says that if Moses had not already received the Torah from the Lord's hand, Ezra would have been worthy to accept it. Israel possessed the Torah, but it was forgotten. Ezra restored its authority and gave it to all the people as a precious possession and guide. Consequently, Ezra is called the second Moses and, like the first, lived to the age of 120.

Ezra was born in Babylon. He was a priest and was descended in a direct line from Moses' brother Aaron. Ezra was also a *sofer*, a scribe; he was called Ezra the scribe. The scribes were the men who, when there were still kings in Israel, acted as royal officials, what we would call secretaries of state or chancellors. They looked after the state archives. In those days only the intelligentsia know how to write, so the word *sofer* became the designation of a learned man. In Babylon there were *soferim* who wrote down and interpreted the holy scriptures and instructed the people in them. It is said of Ezra that he was 'a ready scribe in the law of Moses'. This learned man, who imparted the inherited law to his people with burning zeal, became Judaism's greatest reformer. He set the course that later led, by way of the Pharisees, to the rabbis, who, as compilers of the Talmud, made it possible for the Jewish people to survive.

It was lucky for Judaism that it had more than one centre. The section of the people which went on living in Babylon was far more numerous than the colonists in Judaea. And they followed the developments attentively. Messengers often went between Judaea and Babylon; envoys, relations on visits and pilgrims told the news, and every year a few people broke away from their snug life abroad and travelled 'home' to take part in the reconstruction.

For long ages the news from Jerusalem had been sad and dreary. The first batch of immigrants came to a field that had grown wild, so to speak; they had to cultivate it from the beginning. Solving such a problem was laborious and they had begun late. A few were lucky in business and grew rich. The majority soon became bogged down by poverty, hit by crop failures and burdened with taxes. They sank deeply into debt and became dependent on the rich; the social gulfs cut deep. And the difference between the people and the heathens began to crumble. The danger of the true faith being swept away in the flood of the East's countless religions came alarmingly closer.

A hard core has always survived in Israel. These pious men fought bitterly against the apathy of the time. An echo from them sounds in the last of the prophets, Malachi. He promised that God would intervene and bring new life. 'Behold, I will send my messenger, and he shall prepare the way before me.'

The prophecy was fulfilled; God's messenger was Ezra. The bad news from Jerusalem worked like a summons; he decided to return home. But if his mission was to succeed, he had to come with authority. He cleverly made sure of this. King Artaxerxes gave Ezra a letter which made him judge in Judaea and ordered everyone to obey him. And the king allowed Ezra to leave in the company of 1,500 new immigrants, including Levites and other temple staff, and approved the financing of the expedition.

It was typical of Ezra that he refused a military escort. Instead he ordered the expedition to fast and pray for a successful journey. The expedition started on Nisan 12, the month corresponding to April, and three or four months later, on Ab 1, or August, it reached Jerusalem safely. After three days' rest Ezra handed over his gifts to the temple authorities and showed the Persian commandant his royal authorisation as leader of a thorough religious and social reform.

Ezra realised at once that the situation was even more serious than he had feared. Mixed marriages were the main cause of the trouble. Numerous heathen women had already smuggled in dangerous customs and ideas; their children—

the next generation, the people's future—were on the road
to semi- or complete paganism. It will be remembered that
the marriage contract guaranteed the wife the right to her
own form of worship, and in those days the fertility cult im-
plied the prostitution of both sexes and infanticide.

Ezra, a man of strong convictions, set to work. When
the evening sacrifice in the temple was made, he strode forward, rent his mantle as a sign of sorrow and prayed so loud
that everyone could hear, while he confessed the people's
heresy on their behalf. The learned man's tears and weeping
stirred the multitude. One of the elders began to speak and
acknowledged his own and everyone's faithlessness; he promised that the foreign women should be sent away. Ezra took
him at his word and made the congregation swear that the
promise would be kept.

But a fleeting mood was not enough for him; the evil
went too deep for that. Three days later, on Kislev 20 (De-
cember), Ezra called all the men of Judah and Benjamin
together outside the temple. The winter rain poured down,
the people shivered with cold, 'trembling because of this
matter, and for the great rain' as it says in the Bible. Here
the promise was solemnly renewed and a council appointed
that was to investigate each individual case of mixed marriage, and to arrange divorces. It concerned everybody: the
rich and the priesthood were not to go scot-free. And, in fact,
the council acted quite impartially.

We are witnesses to measures that cut deep. Marriages
were torn in two. Men had loved their wives, lived with
them, seen their children grow up. Now they had to force
themselves to send them back to their families. There was
weeping and wailing in Judaea in those days. But greater
values than personal happiness were involved: the people's
very destiny was at stake.

Such harsh measures had far-reaching consequences. The
expelled women were deeply offended and incited their relations to revenge. Armed men converged on Jerusalem from
all sides. The city was defenceless. It had very few inhabit-

ants. The walls lay in ruins. There was nothing to stop the foreigners from breaking in and destroying and laying waste. Ezra realised that the spiritual wall he had erected round his people was not enough. The capital had to be fortified with a wall of stone. And the task was beyond the people's powers. But just then, at the right moment, the man who saved Jerusalem emerged, and his name stands side by side with Ezra's for all time. It was Nehemiah.

Nehemiah was a distinguished official at King Artaxerxes' court at Susa. His title was cupbearer. In the book in the Bible that bears his name and contains his memoirs, we read that one of his brothers brought sad news from Jerusalem that went to Nehemiah's heart. He put the matter before the king, was given leave and permission to go to Jerusalem. But even more important, the king appointed him temporary regent in Judaea with authority to restore order in the country. Thus equipped, Nehemiah arrived in Jerusalem one spring day in the year 445 B.C.

He stayed incognito for the first three days. At night he rode round the city and inspected the devastated walls and the burnt-down gates. Only then did he introduce himself to the elders and priests. He showed his papers and appealed to the people's patriotism and faith. The walls had to be built. Nehemiah acquired a great following; enthusiastic men streamed in from all over the country and reported for duty. An army of volunteers was mobilised. It was organised in sections, each made responsible for its part of the building.

The difficulties were overwhelming. Formidable enemies had already installed themselves in the city, indeed in the temple itself. They were driven out. And although they plotted and sneered, the work made progress. The classical image of those memorable days is the man with a trowel in one hand and a sword in the other, ready to defend himself. Within two months the wall was finished, defiant and strong. Jerusalem was once again a fortified enclosed town; Judaea had teeth to snap back with.

D

But external security was only the first step on the road. The next task lay behind the walls, sheltered from outside enemies. Nehemiah tackled it. He bridged the gap between rich and poor. In years of drought the poor had been forced to go to the rich for food, but they had had to give security; their fields, vineyards, houses, and even their children no longer belonged to them. Such circumstances created bitterness and unrest. Social reform was badly needed. With the authority the king had given him, Nehemiah suggested that the rich should remit all debts and mortgages. He led the way by his own example. Nehemiah's words and bearing made a deep impression. At a special ceremony the slaves were set free and mortgage deeds given back.

Nehemiah was at the head of Judaea's administration for twelve years and he restored the country to order. But if it was to be firm and lasting, the people had to learn that it was connected with principles that were fundamental in the Torah. And here Nehemiah worked in close co-operation with Ezra. The two men were deeply committed to the belief in God's dominion over Judaea's people, and they dared to set the goal so high that the idea almost makes us reel. They carried out a radical change of the constitution in Judaea. The Torah became the country's constitution.

The two leaders shared the work between them. Ezra looked after the spiritual side of the task, the background for the reform, by spreading knowledge of the Torah. As regent, Nehemiah saw to it that the Torah's doctrines became practical law and were embodied in the legislation.

The year 444 B.C. was the milestone in their work and in Jewish history. On New Year's Day, Tishri 1, people from near and far assembled in front of the Water Gate. Ezra stood on a height and, surrounded by Levites, read aloud the Torah, the draft of the Mosaic books which the scholars at Babylon had drawn up, and which he had brought with him to Jerusalem. The Levites translated and explained the text. The books were, of course, written in Hebrew, so the Levites

repeated them in the Aramaic national tongue. The reading
had a paralysing effect. For the first time each man understood how far he had strayed from the Lord's commandments
in his everyday life. Many sobbed loudly, but Ezra sent them
home with these words:

'Go your way, eat the fat, and drink the sweet . . . for
this day is holy unto our Lord: neither be ye sorry; for the
joy of the Lord is your strength.'

Judaism has always been a joyful religion.

When the heads of families assembled the next day, Ezra
explained the significance of the principal holy-days to them.
Succot, the Feast of the Tabernacles, a harvest festival, which
lasted for eight days, was imminent. Now it was celebrated
with all the ceremonial that was fitting. People built huts
and decorated them with 'the four species': citron, myrtle,
willow twigs and palm shoots. After the Festival, the reading
and explanations began again and the climax was reached
on the 24th of the month.

The day was ordained a day of fasting and mourning.
Long passages from the Torah were read, and everyone confessed their sins and did penance. The Levites preached and
gave colourful descriptions of the people's past in good and
bad times. And when everybody's mind was prepared, the
priests took action. The elders of the people, priests and Levites, signed and sealed a contract in which they bound
themselves on the people's behalf to observe every single
commandment in the Torah, and everyone confirmed the
promise aloud. As fundamental points the document emphasised the ban on mixed marriages, observance of the Sabbath,
letting the land lie fallow every seventh year and offerings
and tithes to the temple officials and the priesthood.

This memorable meeting went down in history as the
Great Assembly. It marked a new phase in Jewish life—the
introduction of the Torah's unconditional sovereignty. It
seemed as if the last of the prophets had handed on his flam-
ing torch to the next generation. For more than two thousand
years it has been passed on from generation to generation.

It goes without saying that such radical reforms could not be carried out all at once. Nehemiah was recalled to his duties in Persia, and when his strong hand was no longer felt, many relapsed. Once more Nehemiah heard black news from Jerusalem and returned yet again. He carried out a sweeping clear-up, banished undesirables and restored order.

History is silent about the centuries that followed. We only know that the consolidation of Judaism progressed with increasing strength. When great world events and catastrophes swept over the country with Alexander the Great and his successors, Judaism showed that it was self-confident. It had the strength to cleanse its own house in the revolt of the Maccabees.

6 / THE TORAH

LATE JUDAISM IS THE TITLE GIVEN TO
Israel's history after the return from Babylon
in many Christian accounts of either the whole
or parts of the period. The words are not well chosen. They
imply that Judaism had passed its peak and was beginning
its last chapter, that it was already fading away. The exact
opposite is the truth. During these centuries Judaism renewed
itself from within and prepared to survive catastrophes in
which any other people would have perished.

People have also spoken of a religious change in Israel.
The fresh defiant creed of the kings and prophets was watered
down into mean-spirited and dry subservience to the law.
Scholars have expressed this by saying that 'Israel's Religion'
gave way to 'Judaism'. But even this assertion does not hold
good on closer examination. The collapse of the state, exile
and homecoming to a task of rigorous reconstruction with
bitter battles to defend what Israel had inherited, and which
made it a unit among the peoples, were hitherto unseen factors that required revolutionary new forms. The answer was
simply that the people's spiritual leaders succeeded in weav-
ing the prophets' teaching into the petty tedious details and
duties of everyday life. They coined the gold into the small
change that was needed if life all the year round and from
morning to night was to be lived in obedience to the God who
had revealed himself through Moses and the prophets to the
people He chose as His own.

Behind expressions such as Late Judaism, which stamped

Judaism as a religion of the law different from the prophets' noble preaching, can be glimpsed the schism between the synagogue and the church. One of traditional Christian theology's eternal clichés makes Judaism retire into isolation and petrify. It slips into the river's foul stationary backwaters and stagnates, while the Church, out in the fresh rushing stream, takes over the Bible's promises and becomes the new Israel. The future belongs to it and sooner or later Judaism must learn to burst the bonds that bind it and rediscover its true self in the Christian church.

This age-old opinion, repeated and emphasised *ad nauseam*, is tragic enough evidence of the very thing the church finds in Judaism: petrifaction. People see only what they care about and need. They put the telescope to their blind eye when looking at things which do not fit into the picture as they would like it to be. That is why the development in Israel during the centuries just before the birth of Christianity is called Late Judaism; that is why the Jewish faith is a deviation from the genuine Israelite creed which Christianity took root in, and later laid hands on, as its legitimate heritage.

But any open-minded person who goes deeply into the period from Ezra up to the turning point of the era, the year zero, soon discovers that during this time the two religions of Judaism and Christianity grew up side by side—faiths that were to survive in the tangled wilderness, with colourful and poisonous flowers, which was the religious world of antiquity. He also finds decisive factors in the development towards the 'Fulness of Time', that wonderful moment for Christians, when the Word became flesh and dwelt among us. The right conditions for the advent of Christianity would never have appeared without quiet and generally unnoticed movements in what is condescendingly called Late Judaism. Anyone who believes that God's hand is behind the course of history will be spellbound as he follows the progress of the greatest drama of all time from act to act.

The scene is set in the little theocratic community around

Jerusalem, the foundations of which were laid by three men
—Zerubbabel, Ezra and Nehemiah. In this small strip of
rocky country between the sea and the Jordan, in this land
of contrasts, which was isolated and yet formed a bridge over
which foreigners passed in friendship or bent on destruction,
they built a wall round the chosen people. Out in the great
world it would have succumbed, infected by destructive
forces. Here it had a few centuries' breathing space in which
it could grow and develop freely until the days of trial came.

All great things have small beginnings. So it was in this
case. Judaea was so small, a pinhead on the map, that it
almost disappeared, first in the mighty Persian empire, then
in Alexander the Great's. Even such an acute historian as
Herodotus does not mention it in his description of the
countries to the east and did not discover its special charac-
teristics. And the first centuries of its history lie hidden in
mist, as corn in the winter earth is hidden under the snow,
while the year goes through its darkest months. But there
was life and strength in it. When history's light shines on
Judaea again, we see its people step forward, numerous
enough to raise an army, firmly established in its faith and
ready to fight for it.

The country was a theocracy, God its invisible but actual
ruler. Therefore the centre lay in Jerusalem's temple with
its religious life. Naturally enough the political head was
the high priest, who was always of Zadok's family. The com-
bination of the spiritual and temporal power in one person
was a protection against the tension and conflicts that are
often seen when the two branches are divided among many
hands. But the high priest was in no sense a dictator; he
shared the power with others. As we know from Ezra's example, the *soferim*, or scribes, were recruited from the priesthood or the educated laymen. Their task was to preserve and
study the holy scriptures and instruct the people. They also
had the responsible task of continuing 'the chain of tradition
of the seventy elders', the oral, unwritten law, to which we

shall return in connection with the creation of the Talmud. We find the essence of the rabbis of later times in the *soferim*. They became not only teachers and lawgivers but also doctors and jurists—marital problems and divorces came within their competence—and lastly preachers.

Most important in the country's government was the big popular assembly, a continuation of what Ezra and Nehemiah had begun and which laid the foundations for the future *Sanhedrin, synedrion* in Greek. The Talmud describes its tasks in these words: 'Be cautious in judging, teach many pupils and set a fence around the Torah.' In other words, it had authority to judge, educate and legislate. Local government was carried out by councils; in villages 'the seven best men' were elected, in towns a 'small sanhedrin' consisted of twenty-three men.

The life of the people these councils, both national and local, had to govern was simple and healthy. Agriculture was the basic occupation. In field and orchard, pasture and vineyard, the people saw God's power call new life to germination and ripening with the changing seasons of the year, and learnt in their prayers to thank Him who gives light and life and in his goodness renews the work of creation every day. Judaea's mountains and valleys began to blossom once again. The dilapidated terraces on the mountain sides were put in order and planted with vines, fig trees and olives; in the fields the corn could be harvested twice every summer; herds of sheep and cattle grazed in green pastures. And every seventh year the fields lay fallow during the earth's sabbath.

The people in the towns were first and foremost craftsmen. A characteristic feature was that not many of Judaea's people were businessmen. The Jew as merchant belongs to his life in exile when trade was almost the only way for him to earn his daily bread. During his classical period in his home country, the Jew was a farmer. In one respect life in Judaea differed from that of other peoples in olden times. Among the latter slavery was the basis of the economic system; the culture of antiquity would have been inconceivable without slaves. In the Jewish community slavery was gradually done away with. The Torah rejected it. Men were free and equal in God's sight; work was not a sign of degradation but had its own natural dignity.

Ezra's work introduced a religious revival. It had already germinated in Babylon, but flowered with strength and vitality when Ezra appeared in Jerusalem. It has always been a rule that revivals begin violently, but that their effect is already on the wane in the second or third generation. The river broadens and loses the original momentum that once hurled it down over steep slopes. But here, too, Israel's people is unique. The religious revival was handed down from generation to generation without diminishing. The synagogue played an important role in this development.

The word 'synagogue' is Greek and so comes from a later period than the one described here. Its original name was *Beth haknesset*, the house of the assembly. We have seen that the institution came into being as early as Babylon. The exiles no longer had the temple, the place in which to worship God. Instead they met for divine service at home or in special houses. Once they had returned to Jerusalem and rebuilt the temple, they preserved the custom. The desire to assemble in small intimate groups was awakened. Fervent prayer and personal devotion found better release here than at the magnificent services in the official temple with a massed choir of Levites and ostentatious sacrifices. Thus *Kehal Chasidim*, the assembly of the pious, found its needs catered for at the synagogue's three daily meetings with songs and prayers. Consequently, the synagogue was also called *Beth hatefilla*, house of prayer.

In our time, nearly one and a half thousand years after those days, the synagogue is still the natural centre of all Jewish life, and the religious rituals are the same as then. Of course, they have undergone a development; the service is more detailed and organised, but the essence of the prayers is the same. The most important are grouped around the *Shema*, the first word of what is closest to a creed in Judaism,

the passage from Deuteronomy 6:4: 'Hear, O Israel: the Lord
our God is one Lord'. The prayers preceding and following
the *Shema* are benedictions of great beauty. One of them has
already been touched on; it has the lovely opening words:

'Blessed art thou, O Lord our God, King of the Universe,
who formest light and createst darkness, who makest peace
and createst all things, who in thy mercy givest light to the
earth and to them that dwell thereon, and in thy goodness
renewest the creation every day continually.'

We have heard about the *Alenu* prayer, which belongs
to the morning service, but the *Amida* or, as it was called
later, *Shemone Esre*, which means eighteen, is also one of the
central prayers. The name was changed when an additional
prayer brought the total to eighteen. It eventually played an
important part in the conflict between synagogue and church.

The synagogue had yet another function, as *Beth hami-
drash*, the house of study. Here the Torah was read and explained, and the common people imbibed its doctrines in
order to put them into practice in their daily lives. Since
Hebrew was no longer the spoken language, the reading took
place in an Aramaic translation, called *Targum*. Here the
soferim found their sphere of activity; with firm and cautious
hands they led the people and protected the revival, from
generation to generation. In some ways the Jews became 'a
kingdom of priests and a holy people', as the Torah enjoins.

The idea of being holy, *kodesh*, was the foundation of
life in Judaea. 'You shall be holy, for I, the Lord your God,
am holy,' it says in the Torah. But holiness has nothing to do
with asceticism; such a concept is alien to the Hebrew Bible.
The varied and specific ordinances which covered both the
ritual rules for priests, Levites and laymen—the so-called
ceremonial law—and moderation, cleanliness and forbidden
foods, aimed at health and strength for the people. The ethical commandments about personal and communal holiness
protected the people from contagion with heathen looseness
and decadence. Hygiene and moderation in the enjoyment of
life's good things always gave the Jews a higher standard of

health than their more primitive and pleasure-seeking neighbours. And the laws about charity, the protection of the small and weak, about justice and social equality, laid stone upon stone in an edifice which was to show that it could stand fast in both good and bad times. Divine worship and everyday life merged in a unity that is characteristic of Judaism. God and ordinary life are not two separate worlds. In Christianity God sometimes seems to be confined in the one and a half hours of the Sunday morning service, while He is apparently forgotten for the rest of the week. The partition between religion and everyday life is broken down in Judaism; religion is a part of daily life, daily life a part of religion. The holy is not profaned thereby, but brought down to earth, and the worldly is transformed into something holy. Like Jesus's mantle, Judaism has no seam; it is woven in one piece from top to bottom.

The Sabbath has always been a source of strength in Israel. It began as a day for rest and family life, but from Ezra's time its spiritual values were emphasised. It was devoted to prayer and study and surrounded with strict ordinances. On the great holidays, especially the festivals of pilgrimage, Passover, the Feast of Weeks (Pentecost) and the Feast of the Tabernacles, the roads to Jerusalem and the temple courtyards were full of singing crowds. The country was so small that nearly everyone could walk to the holy city on these three occasions in the year. But the culmination of the year in the service of God was *Yom Kippur*, the Day of Atonement. If we study the various source books which together make up the Torah, it becomes clear that it was in Ezra's time that Yom Kippur became the crown of the year's offerings for the people's sins and guilt. On this one day in the year's long cycle the high priest went into the Holy of Holies and pronounced the Ineffable Name, and the scapegoat was chased out into the wilderness.

The whole of this rich and varied way of life, which set Israel apart from everything else we know in antiquity, was based on the books in which for centuries the people had stored up their experiences, memories, thoughts and longings, the books which the church has collected in the Old Testament, but which the Jews call the Torah.

The Torah actually comprises only the five Mosaic books that are the foundation of Judaism. The name can also be used of the whole Jewish Bible. But so essential are the books of Moses that it is said that everything in the books of the prophets and the other writings can be found in them. And if the Israelites had not sinned as they did, God would only have given them the Mosaic books.

The word Torah is Hebrew. When the Bible was translated into Greek, the Torah became *nomos*, which means law. Many misunderstandings about Judaism spring from this unfortunate translation. Torah really means much more than law. In reality it cannot be translated by a single word. If one tried to do so, the best answer would be 'teachings'. But what the word implies to the devout Jew is only understood with difficulty by an outsider. It contains an overtone of emotion which makes the believer rejoice. For the Torah is the all-embracing expression of God's revelation, both the written one and that handed down orally. People have tried to express this by saying that the Torah is to the Jew what Christ is to the Christian.

If the idea of the Torah soars to such heights, it goes without saying that in the course of time it was wrapped in legends' colourful veil. Here are some of them. The Torah is perfect and no jot or tittle in it can ever be altered; it is immortal, so long as sun and moon and earth exist. The Torah is older than the world; it existed 947 generations before the creation. Since it is wisdom itself, God took its advice when He created the world. Anyone who dares to deny the Torah's heavenly origin loses his right to life in the world to come. When God gave Moses the Torah, it was, like everything heavenly, of fire, written in black letters on a background of white flames. It was given in the wilderness, because it concerns everybody and the wilderness is a place that no one people has a particular claim on. If it had been given in the land of Israel, the Jews could have refused it to the heathens. And it was issued in fire and water, two elements that everyone has access to. Each letter in the Torah is a living being; the whole world is only a three thousand two hundredth part of the Torah.

I could go on at some length, but that will have to suffice. All these fantasies nevertheless illustrate what a unique position the Torah won for millennia, in both great and small ways, among the Jewish people. That is why the pious Jew finds life's loveliest moments in the study of the Torah. His greatest delight, whether he is young or old, high or low, is reading the Torah. It surpasses everything else, is higher than saving a man from deadly peril, than building the temple, than honouring one's father and mother; a single day's reading is worth more than a thousand offerings. Yes, God himself sits and reads the Torah. Not for nothing does the first psalm in the Bible compare the man who has listened to the Lord's Torah, and ponders over it night and day, to a tree planted by the river which bears fruit and never withers. Everything he does prospers.

This devotion, indeed worship, is the reason why the Torah texts have been preserved intact from the ravages of time. In every generation the *soferim* considered it their life's work to make copies of the Torah, and they subjected every single copy to a strict check. They counted the letters, for they came from God and it was impossible to take too much care. The Talmud simply calls the *soferim* 'letter counters'. In later times they were called *massoretes*, from the word *massor*, to hand down. The result was admirable; today the texts have the same wording as they had 2,000 years ago.

Once he has digested these facts, the reader will understand that the Torah, today as in the past, is sacrosanct in the orthodox Jew's eyes; he is convinced that Moses took down the whole Torah by dictation from Heaven. The results of modern biblical research which even conservative circles inside the church have at long last been forced to recognise, at least partially, are ignored or bitterly contested by orthodox Judaism. As recently as 1964, a distinguished rabbi, Dr. Louis Jacobs of London, had to remove his congregation from the United Synagogue because he held non-fundamentalist views about the Torah's origin, and that learned and distinguished author, Cecil Roth, Professor at the orthodox Bar Ilan University in Israel, was the target for coarse attacks, not because he had actually accepted biblical criticism's ideas about the Torah's origin in his 'Jewish History', but merely referred to them.

To anyone who considers it obvious that the Bible, like every other book from ancient times, has a claim to be put under the microscope of historical criticism, and who believes that God's revelation can certainly withstand such a scrutiny, it seems genuinely shocking to witness such taboos. We must console ourselves by admitting that, when all is said and done, every discussion about biblical research only touches the perimeter. The Bible's actual speech—God's words through it— is undisturbed by discussions about the authors and dates of the individual source books, as well as about who edited them and gave them their final form, and when that happened. However, it is generally agreed that during the centuries we are talking about in these chapters, when *Judaea rediviva* was consolidating itself, the Mosaic books and most of the other books in the Hebrew Bible took the form in which we possess them, and the majority of the canon was provisionally established. It did not become definitive until the second century A.D.

But back to the old, primarily Christian misunderstandings of the Torah, which are rooted in the perhaps not erroneous but inadequate Greek translation of the word that makes Judaism a one-sided religion of the law. We have already seen that the Torah covers far more than simply legal concepts; it contains everything that God reveals about Himself and His will. But in naming God's will we have come to the crux of the matter, where Judaism and Christianity both go their separate ways.

In Israel the emphasis is on *acting* rightly according to God's will, on obeying His commandments. Christianity's central message is man's salvation by God's mercy. A clever theologian has expressed this by saying that Judaism insists on *orthopraxy* and Christianity on *orthodoxy*, the first meaning right action, the second right doctrine. Of course, this is carrying things to extremes. Judaism also has its right doctrine and Christianity does not lack its ethics. Nevertheless, there is an edge in the modern joke about this Jewish characteristic. It tells how one engine of a big jet plane burst into flames in the middle of the Atlantic. The captain warned the passengers of the danger over the loudspeaker; it was so serious that he advised everyone in his own way to prepare for the worst. A Mohammedan threw himself on the floor, turned to Mecca and prayed. The Catholics fingered their rosaries, while they mumbled prayers, and the Protestants sang hymns. The only Jew on board went from seat to seat and collected contributions for a fund which would conduct research into preventing future catastrophes by fire in jet planes!

The truth is that Judaism is not interested in 'salvation', as Christians understand the word, but in doing God's will. Here it should be remembered that the Jew simply does not feel it a burden, much less a laborious duty, to comply with the numerous regulations that govern his life. They all come from God; observing them brings him into contact with God. The more numerous they are, the more frequently they give him the opportunity of doing God's will, and even if many of them seem trivial and niggling, it is not for him to decide what God considers great or small. It is certainly not a question of slavishly following something written, even though it does in truth have divine authority.

It is this Torah, which found its final form when the Jews rebuilt the temple and which the *soferim* guarded so well that today we possess it verbatim, just as Judaea's people heard it when it was read to them in their synagogues, that separates Israel's people from all others. In it lie Israel's dignity and destiny; it is the sign of its election.

7 / ATTACK

IN 334 B.C. ALEXANDER THE GREAT LED HIS
34,000 soldiers over the Hellespont. In speechless amazement the people of the East saw the
new star climb high into the heavens. He seemed to be a
superman, this twenty-year-old Macedonian, who toppled the
mighty Persian Empire with its enormous army at the first
blow of his sword, and in whom military genius was combined
with the mystic's dream of fusing the whole disjointed world
together into one. He dreamed of world dominion and he
won it. By the rule 'Winner take all', the Jews, too, came
under Greek government. Jerusalem did not fight, but sur-
rendered as soon as the king neared the city. We do not know
why. In the past Jerusalem had been a hard nut to crack,
even when formidable enemies were out to win the holy city.
Behind Jewish legend we sense that Alexander treated Judaea
mildly and gave it considerable freedom. Legend has it that
the high priest in ceremonial vestments went to meet the
king at the head of a deputation and handed him the keys
of the city. The king took a liking to these 'barbarians' who
greeted him without abject humility and did not carry idols
with them; indeed, he had seen his reception long before in
a dream. The great king acquired a high place in Jewish
tradition, but his mildness to Judaea was not unique; Alexander always tried to avoid force and to reach his goal peacefully, to disseminate the Greek spirit among the conquered
and make them one people.

With unbelievable speed, almost from one day to another, Alexander had painted new colours on the map of the world. He was one of the rare geniuses who make the great small and the small great in the twinkling of an eye, but even he was mortal. And when a fever carried him away at the early age of thirty-two, everything that he had bound together disintegrated. If the construction of his world empire had been swift, its collapse came even more suddenly. Alexander's generals hurled themselves on the booty like wolves. None of them managed to win it all, but each seized his share. Judaea had to deal with two of the Diadochi (the word means successors): the Seleucids to the north in Syria, with their capital at Antioch, and the Ptolemies, who made Alexandria their capital, in Egypt. As so often before, Palestine lay between two belligerent powers and became a battlefield. After thirty years' bitter warfare, Egypt proved strongest and incorporated Palestine into the Ptolemaic empire for the next two hundred years. On this occasion, too, Jerusalem did not fight, for the Egyptians attacked on a Sabbath, when Jews are normally forbidden to fight.

By and large Judaea had sat in the spectator's seat, while the vast drama of the wars of Alexander and his successors sped by on the universal stage. Very much later we hear an echo of it in the apocalyptic vision in the Book of Daniel, with the fight between the two-horned ram and the goat, the great horn that is broken, and the four more that grow up, each towards its corner of the world, symbols of kings and empires in a life and death struggle.

But when the whirlwind abated, a mist enshrouded Judaea once again and we do not know many details of the two hundred years under Egyptian rule. Nevertheless, behind the calm lurked a tension which gradually grew greater. The Seleucids and the Ptolemies were enemies, to be sure, but in their nature and way of life they were one; their rule was based on Hellenism, their goal to implant it in the mind of every single one of their subjects.

Hellenism is not quite the same as Hellenic culture, but

E

since the last century it has been the name for the mixture
of Hellenic and oriental culture which followed on the heels
of Alexander's conquests and sprang up in the newly founded
'Hellenistic' states. All the old world's Jews, in the home
country and wherever they had taken root abroad, found
themselves suddenly surrounded by the new spiritual climate
and had to take up the challenge.

Today no one thinks anything of the journey from Jerusalem to Athens. An aeroplane does the trip in a couple of
hours. But in olden times Judaea and Hellas lived remote
from each other; neither of them knew the other and each
developed its own pattern of existence. The first book of the
Torah, Genesis, came into being at the same time as the
Greek 'Bible', the Iliad and the Odyssey, and neither of their
creators had any idea of the other's existence. The two cultures consolidated themselves during the same centuries under Ezra and Pericles respectively without the slightest
mutual contact or inspiration. It was not surprising that they
became as different as night and day. In Jerusalem life took
the form of a theocracy; in Athens there was a temporal de-
mocracy, based on slavery, which had little significance in
Judaea. But the contrast became even more glaring when it
came to religion and morality. The Jewish foundation was
the Torah, with its strict monotheism and rules for the whole
of life. In Hellas polytheism ran riot, producing a variegated
mythology whose gods and goddesses were slaves to earthly
desires. One set the holiness of life as the only goal, the other's
aim was life for life's sake, a worship of beauty, art and philosophy for the enrichment of the spirit, the beautiful put
before what a Jew understood by the ethical. In short, the
Greeks believed in the holiness of beauty, the Jews in the
beauty of holiness. If their paths were to cross, sparks would
inevitably result from the clash. The crisis began with Alexander the Great, but it took a few centuries before it became
acute in the form of a bloody struggle.

Before Alexander the Greeks had never tried to spread
their culture among the peoples of the east; they thought it

was too good for the barbarians. Alexander was the first Greek who thought differently. With him the new outlook appeared in the Orient. It taught the people of the east to speak Greek, the language of the classical world, and showed them all its beauty and wisdom. The East did not find it hard to set Zeus up alongside Baal; it leapt and danced joyfully in the Bacchanalian rout of Dionysus and it had long known Aphrodite under the name of Astarte. Perhaps in most places Hellenism did not go far below the surface. It has been compared to a crinoline, which covers a great deal, but does not stir people very much. It reminds us of primitive peoples in modern colonies who gladly adopt European customs, languages, clothes, cars and amusements, all the cheap things, without Europe's real culture penetrating deeply into their minds. Nevertheless, the embrace between Hellas and the East was a warm one, and its results were felt in every corner of the new Greek states. The wind of Hellenism also blew towards Judaism, both at home and abroad; it was on the attack. We shall see where. First of all in Alexandria.

Galut is the Hebrew word for exile, i.e. the Jews in dispersion. But the general designation is the Greek *diaspora*, which simply means dispersion. Most scholars think that it first became general after the destruction of Jerusalem by the Romans in the year 70, but they are wrong. As early as King Solomon's time, Jews lived in distant Spain, and after Samaria's fall and Nebuchadnezzar's conquest of Jerusalem, with deportations of Israelites from both Northern and Southern Kingdoms, Jews were found in many lands to the east. A nucleus took root in Babylon and we know that Jews lived in all the 127 provinces of the Persian Empire. Towards the Christian era the Greek geographer Strabo tells us that Jews lived in all towns and that it would be difficult to find inhabitable places on the earth where 'this tribe' did not live. The Sibylline Books say that every land and every sea was full of Jews. But it was two diasporas that flanked the centre in Jerusalem, the Babylonian and the Egyptian, which in-

fluenced the development of Judaism: the Babylonian centuries after the birth of Christianity, the Egyptian up to the
schism between synagogue and church.

From its infancy Jewish history was interwoven with
Egypt's. We read in the Bible that all three patriarchs,
Abraham, Isaac and Jacob, visited the country, and Hebrew
history proper begins with the bondage in, and liberation
from, Egypt. The wars between the then East and West, in
other words the shifting régimes in Mesopotamia and the
country of the Nile, were waged even in Palestine and drove
both refugees and deportees to Egypt. Under the Ptolemies
Palestine was a vassal to Egypt, with close contacts. The big
country attracted the smaller one. Towards our own era it
is said that 'a hundred myriad' Jews lived in Egypt, in other
words one million out of a total population of between seven
and eight millions. They were not restricted and lived according to their own laws, under their own ethnarch and a council
of seventy members. For centuries they had their own temple,
built on the model of the mother temple in Jerusalem, at
Leontopolis, north of Memphis.

The vast majority of Egyptian Jews had settled in Alexandria, the new colony, which the ruler of the world had
founded and called after himself. Alexandria's five urban
districts were named after the letters of the Greek alphabet.
For example, the fourth, which lay where the Nile ran into
the sea, was called Delta. That is how we get the name for
the land around a river's outlet to the sea. This district and
one other, i.e. two of Alexandria's five quarters, were handed
over to the Jews and were called 'the Jewish sections'. Presumably some hundreds of thousands of Jews lived in the
city. Until not much more than half a century ago no
European or American city could point to a greater Jewish
population.

For many years the big Jewish colony in Alexandria
flourished; it grew rich and influential. Legend still tells us
about the magnificent main synagogue. It was so enormous
that the servants in it had to wave flags when it was time for

the congregation to respond all together with an 'Amen'.

Alexandria was the biggest centre of Hellenistic culture. The Ptolemies lavished their wealth on the city. They built magnificent buildings for academies on the banks of the Nile; here too were the famous library and museum. Scholars from all over the world worked in them to study and instruct bands of disciples. From Alexandria the learning of ancient Greece was spread abroad; its literary and philosophical treasures became available and were sent out to countries everywhere.

This wave of Hellenism also broke over the Alexandrian Jews, and they succumbed to it. Here we witness one of history's first examples of Jewish assimilation, at first cultural, later religious as well. The first symptom of assimilation has always been that knowledge of Hebrew, the language of the Bible, gradually withers away. The Jews in Alexandria naturally spoke Greek, like everybody else. But they also thought in Greek, and the ancient holy tongue slipped into the background. The last word in human wisdom seemed to them to be spoken in Greek. So their Hebrew past had to reconcile itself to the present. Gradually Jewish life in Alexandria embarked on a disastrous course; its aspiration was to explain or at least to justify Judaism to its heathen neighbours. And its spokesmen strove so hard for this goal that they forgot to inform their own people about Judaism and educate them in it. The extensive Jewish literature which blossomed in Alexandria shows signs of this tendency from one end to the other. Characteristic of it is the Greek translation of the Bible, the so-called Septuagint.

Septuagint means seventy, but it ought really to have been called seventy-two. For according to the legend, Ptolemy II, Philadelphus, summoned that number of Jewish scholars, six from each of Israel's twelve tribes, from Jerusalem to Alexandria to translate the Bible. He had each one of them locked up in his own house on the island of Pharos, where they worked completely isolated from one another. When they had finished and the results were compared, they all

tallied miraculously. The reality must have been somewhat
different. Presumably the work went on for a very long time,
but the result is not impressive. The Septuagint teems with
Hebraicisms; at times it is unintelligible to the reader who
does not know the original text. Then, in other places, it
tries to capture the Greek style and so commits treason
against the Biblical method of expression and meaning.

Nevertheless, the Septuagint became a work that won
an enormous circulation and attracted many proselytes.

When the time came, it had prepared the way for the
Christian mission within the Roman Empire; the Jewish
foundation of the Christian faith was well-known to people
through the Septuagint. It goes without saying that orthodox
Judaism was never enthusiastic about the Septuagint. Right
up to modern times the Jews have been chary of translating
the Bible. Translation is superfluous, knowledge of Hebrew
a matter of course and translations become dangerous if they
spoil the original text. The Septuagint did that all too often;
it stands as a monument to Jewish assimilation of heathen
ideas.

Around the Christian era and for some years after it
began, Alexandrian Judaism was the example in the civilised
world of a religion that had moved with the times. Its noblest
figure was the philosopher Philo, who lived at almost the
same time as Jesus. Philo was one of the age's admired popular philosophers, whose efforts were aimed at presenting the
Jewish faith to the heathens as attractively as possible. He
bridged the gap between Greek philosophy and the Bible's
personal and active God by the skilful use of allegorical interpretation. The apostle Paul also makes considerable use of
this method, which gives the imagination free rein. Philo
was an orthodox Jew in obeying the Torah's commandments,
but his philosophical work was a compromise between Judaism and Hellenism. So the Talmud's teachers rejected him;
they do not even mention his name. Inside Judaism Philo is
completely forgotten, but the Christian church remembers
him. In the Gospel according to St. John we find traces of

his teaching about *logos*, the word: 'In the beginning was the word, and the word was with God, and the word was God.' Here the evangelist has taken a lesson from Philo. According to his system, an incorporeal God could not possibly have created the physical world by a direct act. Instead he introduced the connecting link he calls *logos* and which the author of the gospel saw as a symbol of Jesus.

The Jews forgot Philo, and all the splendour he represented vanished. Alexandria's brilliant Judaism with its lofty culture, its organisations, synagogues, wealth and literary stars—all have disappeared. Had it not been for archaeologists' discoveries and scholars' studies of contemporary literature, we should not have known of their existence. They were not wiped out by a catastrophe. Of course, Alexandria's Jews were exposed to antisemitic propaganda, and drastic events befell them. But they were transitory phenomena and no worse than those that happened so often in other places and other ages. Nor was it Islam that destroyed Alexandrian Judaism. It had melted away, so to speak, long before Islam's day. The rapidly growing Christian church certainly absorbed a large part of it, but the answer to the riddle is that it lacked vitality because it had moved away from its original essential character.

Judaism contains eternity in itself. In defiance of all reason it has survived two thousand years of exile. But there were branches on the tree that withered and fell to earth. One of them was once considered to be the most vigorous branch, with the loveliest flowers, but it decayed and disappeared. For it is only the Judaism that remains true to itself that manages to survive. Israel's future was not to be found in the throbbing life between Alexandria's Corinthian columns or among the poets and philosophers representative of the time's refined culture, but in austere and primitive Jerusalem, which began a life and death struggle to defend its heritage just as Alexandria reached its zenith.

Alexandria was the greatest of the many Greek colonial

towns which the great king and his successors scattered throughout their empire. They were important links in the new rulers' attempt to implant Hellenic culture among the barbarians. Their tactics were clever. The goal was not to be reached by the use of power or sudden *coups*, but gradually and by force of example. There lay the new towns, stamped with the Greek outlook on life, with temples, colonnades, academies, sports grounds—some of them even grew up in Palestine. From them Hellenic ideas and customs quietly and imperceptibly infiltrated people's daily lives and thoughts. They even made progress in Judaea. The cultured understood Greek and spoke it. They gave their children Greek names; Joshua became Jason or Jesus, Choni was changed to Menelaus, Eliachim became Alkimos. Jews and Greeks met in the streets of the bazaar; they became friends and went together in the evening to the theatre, the baths or the sports-ground. Intellectuals studied Greek philosophy. Pious Jews looked more severely on this than if a man was a regular visitor to a courtesan. For she could only infect the body, but the former poisoned the mind.

Perhaps this peaceful infiltration of the Jewish mentality by the Greek spirit would have undermined Israel, had not a brutal tyrant suddenly torn off his mask when in obstinate impatience he tried to pluck Judaism up by the roots to make way for the paganism of Hellenism. He showed the Jews its real face and the catastrophe aroused the people to the struggle that legends never tire of depicting. His name was Antiochus Epiphanes; the nickname means the Glorious, by implication, god, but the people wittily changed it to Epimanes, the Madman. And it was not inappropriate.

Palestine had been a bone of contention between the Seleucids and the Ptolemies for centuries, but in the year 198 B.C. the King of Syria decisively wrested the country from Egypt's hands. A couple of decades later Antiochus Epiphanes ascended the throne and began his disastrous course of action. Few foreigners have had such a radical influence on Israel as this prince. He became a religious archetype. The church borrowed features from him in its description of Antichrist. Antiochus was born in Athens and never forgot that he was once chosen to be chief in the city at the foot of the Acropolis. Filled with admiration for Hellas, he was firmly determined to clear the way for Hellenism and 'to civilise' his dominions. In his way he was a benevolent man, but foolish and anxious to please. He represented the bad side of the Greek spirit and its behaviour to conquered nations. Through him pagan arrogance profaned what was holy in Palestine. But Antiochus had the excuse that there were Jews in Jerusalem who summoned him and asked him to give their people the blessing of Greek culture.

Only a small minority of the Jews in Jerusalem had allowed themselves to be swept away by the tidal wave of Hellenism. But it was they who had influence and power. Convinced that the new culture had the future before it, they asserted that if the Jews were to find a place in it, they must give up the customs that made them 'different': the observation of the Sabbath, circumcision and the laws about forbidden foods. Without paying the slightest attention to the means they used, they succeeded by bribery and intrigues in getting one of their own party appointed high priest. He was certainly not a cohen, a priest of Aaron's stock, as had always been the invariable rule. But the king supported him with a Greek garrison in David's citadel in the capital; he was to be the instrument for wiping out Judaism and incorporating this refractory people into 'the one people' of Antiochus' kingdom.

The process of Hellenisation gathered momentum; nothing was neglected to transform Jerusalem into a Greek city. A stadium was built at the foot of the citadel, where young men took part in athletics and competitions naked, as was the Greek custom, thereby violating the time-honoured Jewish sense of modesty. They had even undergone operations for removing the marks of circumcision. Race-courses and theatres beckoned; Dionysian and Bacchic processions, joyous, noisy and abandoned, had a free passage through the holy city. The devout drew back in horror.

But it did not go fast enough. After a series of disturbances Antiochus decided to Hellenise the obstinate Jews systematically and forcibly. He issued a proclamation ordering everybody in his realms, without exception, to renounce their own religion and bow down to the Greek gods instead. The edict was accepted peacefully enough in other countries, but it aroused consternation in Judaea, for it meant that the Torah, the country's fundamental law, was annulled. The blow was directed at Judaism's heart. Suddenly it was the death penalty for circumcision, celebrating the Sabbath and abstaining from forbidden foods, and even for reading the Torah. The temple services were suspended and the rule of fear reached a climax on the day when an altar to Zeus Olympius was installed in the temple itself and everyone was compelled to sacrifice on it. This was 'the abomination of desolation in the holy place'. Zeus had ascended Yahweh's throne.

Now that the goal had been reached, even the most ardent progressives began to retreat. Antiochus had attacked what everyone in Judaea had been taught from childhood was the holy of holies. In this hour of need an unknown author wrote the Book of Daniel, and its visions and promises flew from mouth to mouth. The book has indeed the ring of the old prophets; it gave people courage to hold out. Its words did not sound in vain; these years became the period of martyrdom in Israel. The Jews showed the world that in bad times not only could specially endowed personalities suffer death for an idea, but also that a whole people could sacrifice what they possessed and go through torture and death to remain faithful to what they considered holy and true. A striking example was Hannah, who saw her seven sons murdered and the skin flayed off them because they refused to eat pork as a sign that they renounced their faith. Their mother inspired them to say 'no' and die. Finally she herself was killed. For centuries the Jews had bowed to foreign masters.

Now their ancient pride and faith awoke; nationalistic and pious Jews found one another on the same side. Only a spark was needed to send the barrel of gunpowder flying in the air. That happened in a little village called Modiin on the day when an old priest, Mattathias, together with his five sons, cut down a fellow-countryman because he was sacrificing on the altar of a false god. The revolt of the Maccabees exploded and a war that was against all commonsense began; the weak against the strong, the few against the many. And the weak and the few conquered in a campaign they waged under the device:

'*Mi kamocha ba'elim adonai*, Who is like thee among gods, O Lord?'

8 / THE MESSIAH

HELLENISM'S ATTACK ON JUDAISM HAD been like a dangerous illness, a virus that infected the body of the people. Its poison had not been without effect; contagion always destroys something, even in the healthiest body. But the revolt of the Maccabees showed how much strength Israel had gained through centuries of quiet growth. To continue with the simile of an illness: the white corpuscles were mobilised and brought the infection to a speedy conclusion. Nevertheless, the healing process left its traces behind; true, the patient survived the illness, but the forces it aroused and which brought Israel through the crisis simultaneously created changes that were to have their effect on the history of the world. The next 300 years not only saw Judaism develop and finally take shape as the entity it was to be for thousands of years, but they also saw the foundation laid from which a new universal religion, Christianity, grew up. In truth, the Maccabees set up one of the great milestones in the history of mankind.

The revolt broke out in defence of the country's religion. But the motives of the rebels were not all identical, and when victory was assured, their ways parted. Mattathias and his sons fought as much for national as for religious freedom. Their goal was to build up an independent and strong Jewish state in which the people could obey the Torah and worship God in the fashion of their fathers without having to ask a foreign ruler's permission first. But as the years went by and the goal was reached, political and national considerations increasingly outshone religious ideas. Maccabean sovereignty lost its brilliance; its kings degenerated into rough soldier-princes, who looked grotesquely out of place in their high priests' vestments and aroused the contempt of the devout in the country.

For these devout men, or *Chasidim*, as the Hebrew word goes, freedom meant freedom to serve God. They had taken up arms only under compulsion; they had hurled themselves into battle only when there was no alternative. Then they had stood side by side with the Maccabees and fought with the bravest of the brave. But as soon as victory was in their hands and religious freedom guaranteed, they all agreed to seek peace and to return to a quiet life of studying the Torah and obeying its commandments. They withdrew from the struggle and let the country's powerful men continue it. But the devout, too, had their divisions. The name *Chasidim* gradually disappeared and was replaced by Pharisees and Essenes, the two sects into which the devout split up.

'The Pharisee is a hypocrite.' No Christian is startled if he hears that assertion. For it is generally accepted that Pharisaism and hypocrisy are identical. Under the word 'Pharisee', many dictionaries simply give 'hypocrite' as the equivalent. And one has only to listen to a few preachers in European churches to realise that the two words are used indiscriminately and that one of the cheap clichés that flows easily and naturally into their flood of rhetoric is a warning against Pharisaic behaviour. No one in the congregation reacts or protests, for that is the sort of thing they learnt in the Bible classes of their distant schooldays. It is part of the doctrine of the faith of their childhood.

We shall soon see how distorted this generalised picture of the Pharisees is. But it must be admitted that teachers, clergymen and congregations are comparatively innocent when they look down on the Pharisees, giving them a wide berth for their souls' salvation and taking great care not to

be like them. For they have been indoctrinated with, and
have uncritically accepted, the four Gospels' description of
the Pharisees without realising that they have thereby been
pushed into the Christian front ranks in the thousand-year-
old conflict between synagogue and church, where all nuances
disappear and there is only room for black and white.

Even a superficial reading of the New Testament leaves
the impression of sharp clashes between Jesus and the Pharisees. They stand, and not without reason, as dangerous
enemies of the authors of the Gospels, and the Bible teems
with attacks on them. We read that Jesus reproached them
for preaching what was right without practising it themselves.
They did good deeds in order to be seen; they made their
phylacteries broad and the borders of their garments big;
they gave tithes of mint and anise and cummin, but neglected
the important commandments in the law about justice and
pity; they strained at the gnat, but swallowed the camel
whole and were whited sepulchres, outwardly clean, but in-
wardly full of rottenness and filth. And this long list of
accusations is only an extract from a whole lexicon of the
Pharisees' sins and shortcomings.

Later on we shall look at the Gospels' value as source
books for the life-history of Jesus; here we would simply point
out that, in addition to a great deal else, they were polemics,
weapons for both attack and defence, during the period when
the young church was extricating itself from the swaddling-
clothes of Judaism, and therefore cannot be regarded as im-
partial evidence. But it must also be remembered that it has
always been possible to direct similar criticism against even
the noblest spiritual movements. There has never been a
new movement in which, as time went by, the first and greatest man did not recede into the background, while number
two worked his way forward into the front rank, because
hollow echoes mutilated and distorted what had once been
great and fine. It was not the cause itself that became less
splendid, but its own advocates who tarnished it. Not long
after the death of Jesus his teaching suffered the same fate.

What would be our reaction if Christianity were to be judged, not by its founder or the martyrs who gave their lives for it, not to mention the countless anonymous men who lived it out in their daily lives and died blissfully in the faith, but by hypocritical and mendacious princes of the church, who exploited religion's organisations and used them for their own advancement? A religion is entitled to be judged by the best it has to give and not the worst.

Judaism itself had a sharp eye for black sheep among the Pharisees. Thus the Talmud enumerates seven kinds of Pharisees and subjects the first five to devastating criticism. Let us take a look at all seven of them. They are:

1. 'The shoulder-Pharisee', who boastfully carries his good deeds on his shoulder for all to see.

2. 'The wait-a-moment Pharisee', who postpones helping his injured neighbour until he has finished the pious prayer he is in the middle of.

3. 'The bruised Pharisee', so called because he bangs his head against a wall when looking back at a pretty girl and hurts his face.

4. 'The pestle Pharisee', who walks about with head bowed down like a pestle in a mortar.

5. 'The calculating Pharisee', who works out the good deeds with which he can make up for his sins of omission.

The words the Talmud uses to describe these five groups are not friendly ones; it calls them 'world destroyers' and says they are a 'pestilence'. But the Talmud also recognises the good Pharisees. There are two types of these, forming numbers six and seven: 'the god-fearing Pharisee', who is like Job, and 'the Pharisee who loves God' and is like Abraham.

But leaving all that aside, we can draw a more accurate picture of the Pharisee if, without preconceived opinions and keeping our eyes open, we make a careful study of the sources that have survived two thousand years of wear and distortion. The name Pharisee comes from a Hebrew verb *parash*. The word can be translated as 'to interpret' and indicates that the Pharisees, like the *soferim*, expounded the Torah and educated the people in it. But the word also means 'to differ from' and that is certainly the translation that characterises the Pharisees best.

In Judaism there was nothing unusual about someone wanting to 'be separate'. The Torah's many detailed provisions do in fact make distinctions, namely between the clean and the unclean. The idea behind this was to help men to attain the degree of holiness that is necessary in order to have communion with God.

Distinction. That is the word that comes to mind when we want to characterise the Pharisees. The distinction between clean and unclean in life's tremendous variety. First and foremost, distinction from things foreign. As a result of Hellenism, foreign influences, both good and bad, had affected the Jewish people. Here the Pharisees kept careful watch. One of their main tasks was to keep the people at a safe distance from forbidden ground. The detailed, to us often far-fetched, regulations they taught acted as a fence, an insurmountable wall between Jew and heathen. Naturally it was only a short step from that to sophistry and hairsplitting, which made great things small and small things great, to what is known as casuistry—and it cannot be denied that the step was taken.

At the boundary stood the Torah; it marked the frontier between the chosen people and the heathens. But the Torah had been given many centuries ago. And times change; they are never the same. Therefore it was incumbent on each new generation to interpret the Torah, so that men in every age could know God's will in the contemporary situation. And these interpretations were handed down from generation to generation. They were not written down, but remembered, and well remembered. Every single detail had to be preserved, for each one contained God's will. So teachers and pupils developed their memories to a fantastic degree. The ideal was to be like an asphalted well that does not lose a drop of water. Thus, side by side with the written Torah there developed an oral Torah, or, as it is also called, 'the chain of tradition of the elders'. A long time afterwards it was written down and called the Talmud. It was this oral Torah in which the Pharisees instructed the people, and they conferred on it the same divine authority as the written Torah, which was created under God's guidance. We can say that the Pharisees were the modernists of the age; they made possible a flexible adjustment of the Torah so that it remained up to date.

But the picture of the Pharisees first acquires real colour when we compare them with their opposites in Jewish life around the birth of Christianity. Pharisees and Sadducees: the two words are automatically spoken in the same breath by the man who remembers the biblical history of his childhood. And yet they represent two extremes; indeed one can almost say that there was a gulf between them. True enough, both sects were Jews; the Sadducees insisted on the fundamental importance of the Torah as much as the Pharisees. But only of the written Torah; they rejected the oral law. That was only one of many differences between the two.

The Sadducees were named after Zadok, the high priest in King Solomon's day. That immediately indicates that they were the aristocracy in Israel. The high priest was chosen from them until the Maccabean kings themselves took over the office. The centre of the Sadducees' life was the temple, with its sacrificial services. They were to be found among the priesthood. Gradually, as the high priests became transformed into temporal princes, the Sadducees became the real nobility in Israel; they had political influence and held the high offices. They were conservative in religious matters and opposed all innovations, and they rejected the belief in another world and the resurrection of the dead.

The contrast between the two tendencies is now clear. The Sadducees valued an aristocracy of the blood; the Pharisees created an aristocracy of learning. And whereas the Sadducees looked after the temple's interests, the Pharisees introduced the people's spiritual life into synagogue and home.

F

For them true divine service was not primarily sacrifice, but prayer and study of the scriptures. The future belonged to the Pharisees. With the destruction of the temple in the year 70, the Sadducees received a death blow; their school disappeared for ever from Jewish life.

The Pharisees never became numerous. There were only a few thousands of them at the most, but they were active and acquired widespread influence among the people. This did not mean that their teaching reached everybody. On the periphery of the people were the *am ha'aretz*, whom the Pharisees despised as the rough ignorant masses Jesus called sheep without a shepherd. Many of them found in him what the Pharisees had not been able to give them. Nevertheless, spiritual life awoke in synagogues and home wherever the Pharisees went. We picture them as over-scrupulous and grim. And so they could be when religious life entered the danger zone. Yet the verse in the Psalms, 'Serve the Lord with gladness', gives a better idea of them. Their attitude to life was positive and healthy; asceticism had no part in their creed. It is to their credit that they made home life richer. Especially by making woman the centre of the home, they gave her dignity as defender of family peace. They also taught her to turn the Sabbath into the day that delights and uplifts. They literally did this by entrusting her with the task of lighting the candles when the Sabbath began. It is significant that the only Maccabean monarch who was not hostile to the Pharisees was a queen.

Long lists of names of great teachers among the Pharisees are remembered in Jewish tradition. One of the greatest was Hillel. He lived at the beginning of our era and was praised for his prodigious learning and the clear interpretations and answers he always gave. His imperturbability provoked a man to wager that he could throw Hillel off his balance and make him angry. Just before the Sabbath he knocked on the door and disturbed Hillel in his bath with a foolish question. A couple of minutes later he repeated the process, then he did it a third time. But every time he asked he received a thorough answer that showed no sign of annoyance. At last the stranger lost his self-possession and complained loudly that he had lost his wager. Hillel's answer was: 'It is better to lose a wager than one's patience.'

Once a heathen asked Hillel to summarise the Torah in so few words that he could say them while standing on one leg. His answer is well-known; it was: 'Do not unto your neighbour what you would not that he should do unto you.' These words are called the golden rule. A generation later Jesus took this saying up and formulated it in a positive form. He wanted everybody to treat his neighbour as he wanted his neighbour to treat him. It is arguable whether this is an improvement. Men are very different, and it is by no means certain that my neighbour has the same tastes as I have. If certain persons, and they do exist, interfere in other people's affairs, with the best will in the world or because they want to attract attention, the result can be embarrassing and smack of meddlesomeness. Reserve is also a good rule, therefore some of us should be allowed to prefer the golden rule of the ancient Pharisee.

By now we can see that the Pharisees are simply not the symptom of decadence beloved by contemporary ecclesiastical caricature. Pharisaism must not be regarded as the dark background to the clear light of the Gospel, but as a religious school with strong forces hidden in it. And it was the Pharisees who brought Judaism safely out of the catastrophes that awaited it. It has been said that Judaism itself stands as a monument to Pharisaism, and it is no exaggeration.

But it was also among the Pharisees that resistance lay ready to spring up when Jesus began his ministry.

Judaea's desert is the land west of the Dead Sea, a wild and stony region where shattered cliffs are broken up by gorges and there are no roads and no water, just stone after stone, and a pitiless sun shining overhead from morning to night. If you have ventured into this lunar landscape, you cannot believe your eyes when you suddenly find yourself in Ein Geddi, a green fertile valley, with purling springs and houses and busy people. The contrast is so violent that it shocks you. And yet Ein Geddi is no *fata morgana*, but reality. It exists today and it existed 2,000 years ago. Here lived the remarkable Essenes, about whom we know far too little and yet enough to guess that they helped to plough the soil in which Christianity's seed was to germinate.

We do not even know why they were called Essenes. Perhaps the name indicates that they were devout, perhaps that they were silent, perhaps that they bathed. At any rate, all three things form part of their picture. But the most important is that the Essenes withdrew from the world and sought solitude. The Sadducees and Pharisees went out into the restless fermenting life of every day and tried to influence people with their ideas. But the Essenes were the forerunners of Christian monasticism. Ever since their time there have been men who, as if acted on by some centrifugal force, are driven out of the community to keep away from temptation and win peace of mind in isolation together with other like-minded people. Ein Geddi was one of their centres, but they also built villages in other places and lived their monastic life wherever they were given permission to observe the Torah's every regulation undisturbed. They have been called Pharisees in the superlative.

The Essenes were industrious farmers; they worked from morning till night. The day began and ended with bathing, prayer and silent contemplation. They created a utopia with equality and fellowship in everything, a model for the first Christian community in Jerusalem and much later for Tolstoy's ideas or the positive values in Socialism and Communism. Most of them were celibate; the few who married practised a minimum of sexual intercourse with their wives, just enough to increase the community's birthrate. The Essenes were undoubtedly pacifists, but if the country was in danger they took up arms, as they did under the Maccabees and later during the war against the Romans, and stood together with their people.

New light may possibly be thrown on the life and ideas of the Essenes by the discovery of the Dead Sea Scrolls and the monastic buildings at Qumran. Qumran lies near Ein Geddi, and close study of the age-old crumbling parchments' account of the War of the Sons of Light against the Sons of Darkness and especially the handbook, the Manual, about the daily discipline of life in the monastery, may eventually provide scholars with information about these remote figures. There are grounds for the claim of some scholars that John the Baptist spent years of quietness and preparation for his call among the Essenes at Ein Geddi or in the brotherhood at Qumran. Perhaps James, our Lord's brother, was himself an Essene. In any case, he seems to have lived the life of a monk and an ascetic, as they did. By paths, the traces of which have been obliterated by the millennia, the Essene's ideas may have found their way into men's minds and opened the door for Jesus's message. The Essenes form part of the many-coloured picture presented by Judaism just before the Fulness of Time. The passage from the Psalm, '. . . them that are quiet in the land', refers to them, and so do Jesus's words about 'the meek, who shall inherit the earth'. Two apt quotations with which to close our account of them.

The Maccabees made the country great; they built a Jewish Palestine. No one would have thought it possible that a people who for centuries had been humble vassals of foreign rulers had the strength not only to burst the bonds that bound them and free themselves, but also to extend their frontiers and end up as a power that even Rome had to reckon with. The dramatic events with war's alternating moments of pride and bitterness, the bravery and contempt for death that adorn the Maccabees' saga, have no place in this book. The reader can find them in the Books of the Maccabees. But the Lilliputian state of Judaea had suddenly become great. The Maccabean monarchs conquered not only Galilee, Samaria and the Philistines' towns, but also the lands of Moab and Edom. The kingdom extended over most of Palestine and at times was bigger than David's empire.

The newly conquered districts were made Jewish. Jews settled in them and the original inhabitants were converted to Judaism. Not voluntarily, but by force. If anyone dared to oppose conversion, he was killed. That is one of the shadows over the Maccabees' rule. There can be no defence of a people that had complained bitterly of religious persecution becoming adepts at it themselves. But that is what happened. And the recent converts became genuine Jews; indeed their descendants prided themselves on being Jewish. Moreover, it can be asserted that had it not been for these conversions the Jewish people would have been absorbed by its heathen neighbours and Jewish life and religion only known through archaeological discoveries. Those were times when the sword had the last word. In any case, the bloody brutal twentieth century has certainly nothing to learn from antiquity when it comes to oppression and coercion.

The rule of the Maccabees degenerated. The brilliance of its emergence into history was matched only by the completeness of its ultimate degradation. Forcible conversions were a symptom of spiritual decline. They corresponded to the gradual secularisation of Judaea's policy. Soon the monarchs' interests were solely concentrated on armies, war and diplomatic negotiations. The theocracy slowly turned into a despotic monarchy; the kings became the high priests and controlled the temple. A cultural conflict began to ferment. The Sadducees sided with the state; the Pharisees took the opposite point of view. The country enjoyed peace only for short periods. Although no enemies threatened from without, rebellion and unrest were rife among the people and countless Pharisees were murdered because of their faith. It all ended in civil war. This was nothing new in Israel's history. Right down from Cain and Abel's day fraternal hatred leaves its bloody trail: Isaac and Ishmael, Jacob and Esau, Solomon's victory over Adonijah. The last Maccabean kings were the brothers Hyrcanus and Aristobulus, who hated and intrigued against each other. Neither of them noticed the thundercloud which darkened on the horizon ready to discharge its wrath on Judaea.

In comparison with Israel, Rome was an upstart. Legend says that its founders, the twins Romulus and Remus, were suckled by a wolf. Whether the story is true or not, Rome was founded during the years when Isaiah was writing his immortal book in the kingdom of Judah. But it was written in the book of fate that the sturdy barbarian state on the Tiber should grow to manhood and inherit the world. While the kingdom of the Maccabees drifted to its downfall, Pompey and his legions swept victoriously through Asia Minor and Syria, and Rome stretched out its tentacles to Jerusalem. With criminal naiveté both Maccabean brothers appealed to him and asked for help. Pompey did not wait to be asked twice and attacked. In the year 63 B.C. he incorporated Judaea into the Roman Empire. Pompey dishonoured the temple and entered the holy of holies. He had expected to find the Jews' god inside, for everyone knew that it was an ass nailed to a tree. But the room was empty, for the true God is invisible. The Romans never learnt to understand that. But from that moment Rome's sword hung over the Jews. The day was to come when it would strike, shattering and splitting them.

The Maccabees' period of power covered a century in Israel's history. They liberated Jerusalem in 165 B.C.; 102 years later Pompey enslaved the holy city once again. But this century of freedom had not been a tranquil idyll. The revolt against the Syrians continued for twenty-five years and took a great toll before the victory was won.

And during the rest of the period the annals are packed with accounts of campaigns and civil war; there are bloodstains on nearly every page. And Rome did not bring peace. The conquest of Jerusalem was the signal for veritable orgies of blood. Descendants of the defeated Maccabees tried desperately to win back the lost throne. The family's re-

nown was still bright in the people's minds and they had a
large following. They fought like wild beasts against the
legions' trained soldiers. Confusion was worse confounded
by the Roman civil war. Palestine changed rulers four times;
each upheaval meant men killed in battle and death afterwards for the defeated. Finally Herod stepped forward out
of the confusion. Changing rulers in Rome gave him the
power he thirsted for.

When Herod became king, the country was like a wilderness; more than 100,000 Jews had been killed. And these
dead had been the people's finest sons, young patriots who
had refused to bow their necks under the foreign yoke. The
survivors hid in Galilee, far from the centre of the state in
Jerusalem. Decades later new rebels, the so-called Sicarii or
Zealots, swarmed forwards from their ranks. But Judaea's big
popular rising did not come until much later. Nevertheless,
dread of it oppressed the new king's distrustful mind like
a nightmare.

Destiny has its ironical smiles. One of them lights up
evilly when mention is made that Herod, the most hated
and despised of the Jews' kings, was an Idumaean; in other
words, he had roots in one of the compulsorily converted
peoples. But no one considered him as any more than a half
Jew; popular wit called him the Idumaean slave. The Jews
saw in him the representative of the Rome they loathed. An
ancient historian says that 'he stole his throne like a fox,
ruled like a tiger and died like a dog'. But equally spiteful
words have been said about other kings. It is true that permanent distrust drove him to ravage like a wild beast that
rends what it fears. The list of his victims is endless. As a
gardener weeds the garden, Herod cleared court and family
of everybody on whom even the shadow of suspicion fell,
first and foremost the family of the Maccabees, including
his own queen. In order to win over the people he had
married Mariamne of the former royal family and loved her
passionately. But he had her strangled. His two sons suffered
the same fate with her. When he heard the news, the Emperor

at Rome burst out: 'I would rather be Herod's pig than his son.' The point of the remark is that Jews never touch a pig. It is doubtful if there is any truth in the story of the children's murder in Bethlehem, although it would be in keeping with his other actions. Before his death he ordered one member of every outstanding family in the country arrested. As soon as he was dead, they were to be murdered. He wanted there to be sorrow in the kingdom, if not for his own death, then for theirs. But in the Jewish tradition the day of his death is celebrated as a day of rejoicing.

It was the foreigners, the Greeks and Romans, who called Herod 'the Great'. Among them he sought the renown his soul aspired to. He could cringe before the mighty in Rome, but he was more astute than they. It is incredible how often in hopeless situations he was able to twist and turn so that he emerged from his dilemma unscathed, and landed on his feet like a cat. A personality of unusual dimensions, embracing the base and the lofty, was housed in this powerful muscular warlike figure. And he created masterpieces of stone, if not of men: Caesarea, on the Mediterranean, and the fortress of Massada, which has recently been excavated, to name two examples. A brilliant stroke was the reconstruction of the temple, which had been badly damaged by the constant ravages of sieges and conquests. In this he had an eye to winning over the Jews, regardless of the tremendous expense. He erected the white and gold building high on the mountain; it shone in the sun like a wonder of the world. 'He who has not seen the temple at Jerusalem does not know what beauty is,' was a popular saying in the country.

Herod ruled for more than thirty years. His anxiously awaited death occurred a few years after Jesus was born. In accounts of this central period in the world's history it is often overlooked that the background to the emergence of Christianity was unparalleled political and social chaos and terror in the country in which the Almighty gave us his only begotten son. Yet it is essential to a correct understanding of the schism between Judaism and Christianity to emphasise the insecure conditions in Palestine around the beginning of the Christian era.

Herod had named three of his sons as heirs in his will. It was to be a long time before any of them sat firmly in the saddle. The country collapsed into indescribable anarchy and chaos. One of Herod's sons had 3,000 visitors to the temple killed in the sacred edifice itself and their bodies piled up in heaps next to the sacrificial animals. The great revolt, which ended in the burning of Jerusalem seventy years later, actually broke out as early as this. In Galilee the Zealots ventured out of their caves and cut down royal and Roman soldiers wherever they found them. Their leader was Judah the Galilean, who is mentioned in the New Testament. He had seen his father murdered by Herod's underlings and inherited nothing but bitterness and hate. Judah set Galilee aflame. I wonder if readers of the gospels, who have been stuffed with charming legends about Jesus's idyllic childhood, realise that the same Judah's headquarters lay only an hour's march from the Nazareth where Mary brought up her son. The Roman general Varus, who crushed the revolt and crucified thousands of the conquered, was the same Varus who met his death in the Teutoburg forest in battle against the German barbarians, he whom Augustus Caesar invoked with the words: 'Varus, Varus, give me back my legions.'

Divide et impera, divide and rule. So ran one of Rome's tested principles, if anyone dared to bid defiance. So the Senate upheld Herod's testament and gave him not one, but three successors. But Rome could not leave a powder barrel watched solely by native princes. The days were long past when Judaea had been an unimportant patch in a remote corner of the map. It had strategic importance and shared frontiers with the Parthian empire with which Rome was perpetually at war, but never conquered. On top of that, Judaea was the national and religious centre for the many Jews dispersed throughout the empire, with influence in many quarters. The Senate appointed a procurator as the highest authority with his seat at Caesarea. The position was held by a series of men who ruled with a chill and iron hand and used their opportunities to make their fortunes in the occupied country. One of them was Pontius Pilate. Two thousand years after those days his name is still heard whenever a Christian says the creed: 'Suffered under Pontius Pilate.'

Rome and Jerusalem never learnt to understand each other. In the Jews' eyes Rome was the godless barbarian world power which a Jew had to keep away from and beware of. With watchful hatred Israel waited for an opportunity to win back its precious freedom; the Zealots sharpened their knives. And Rome was on guard. In every protest and complaint about images in the temple or the building of theatres and circuses, or about new taxes, the procurators saw the germs of revolt. The only answers they had to give were severity and brutality and fresh extortion. As the years went by, events moved towards their appalling climax with the inexorability of a Greek tragedy. The conflict inevitably burst into flames. Rome took four years to put the fire out. Not until Jerusalem was laid waste did peace fall over the shattered land. But the embers smouldered; sixty-two years later they again burst into flames, which went on glowing until the kingdom's end. Rome had to employ all its resources to crush the Son of a Star's desperate rebellion. But then the last Jew was driven out of the land of his fathers. For exactly 300 years, from 165 B.C. to A.D. 135, Palestine was a battlefield.

Christianity grew in a field that was watered with Jewish blood.

In the midst of these centuries' confused mixture of desperation, lamentation and sheer defiance, a longing sprang up that the Almighty would intervene and in a flash transform sorrow into joy and defeat into victory. This was a belief that was old in Israel, but never had the people needed it as they did then. It was the belief in the Messiah and his kingdom.

But the moment we mention the word 'Messiah', we stand on the edge of the impassable gulf that forms the barrier between Judaism and Christianity. Jew and Christian each stand on their own side and are unable to call to each other. The Christian has found the Messiah. He once lived on this earth and the Christian faith looks back to the time when God revealed His salvation through him. But the Jews look forward to him who has not yet come, but will come one day. The Jew's mind is dominated by the unshakable conviction that the divine impact on the world's history lies not in the past, but in the future. One day the Lord's chosen people will experience its great age. Therefore their thinkers, bards and prophets are always on the look-out; they shield their eyes with their hands, ever peering ahead for a sign of what will happen in God's own time. But the night is long and dark, and they must wait and wait until the distant day finally dawns.

Neither before nor since has expectation seethed and bubbled over in people's minds as it did around the time of Jesus's coming. In peaceful pleasant times people are content with imitation jewellery, instead of real pearls. When catastrophes cast their sinister flickering gleams over a frightened generation, they grope for supports that will really hold. It is in storms and foul weather that the helmsman steers by the light that shows him the way.

The core of the Messianic idea is the conflict, the eternal conflict, between dream and reality. In this tragic clash, steel met flint and the sparks flew far and wide through the land. For everything turned out quite differently from what the Jews had been promised. The prophets had foretold great days for Israel. The nations' wealth was to be brought with their kings as leaders; the sons of the oppressors were to bow down, and everybody who had scorned Israel throw themselves at its feet. But the brutal reality was slavery under foreign rulers; instead of bearing gifts, godless Roman procurators plundered the chosen people; the son of David had not shown himself, only the Idumaean Herod and his sons. But no, among the dark clouds could be seen the fitful glimmer of a star that was a presage of the future, in spite of everything. Misfortunes have their day, but the Messiah was to sweep them all aside. And the day was near.

Messiah is a Hebrew word that means the anointed one. Translated into Greek—the language the New Testament is written in—Christos. The reference is to the kings of Israel who were anointed before they took over the government. And this future king was the man who was to usher in the great age. He was to be of Judah's tribe, of David's line and was to come from Bethlehem, David's town. His time had been foretold by Elijah. To this day one chair is left empty at the table in Jewish houses during Passover mealtimes. If Elijah were to come to any Jewish house at that time, he would find himself expected. In another version, the Messiah's harbinger was a king, who conquered Jerusalem, but was crushed by the world powers Gog and Magog, or, as others said, by an enemy called Armilius, a distortion of Romulus. Angels concealed his body together with those of the patriarchs, and not until the Messiah came would he win the great war and create peace on earth.

A long series of remarkable writings appeared and went from hand to hand. They were constantly read and retold; everyone heard of their fantastic and encouraging reports. We call these literary offshoots of the Messianic idea Apocrypha and Pseudepigrapha, and we get our knowledge of it through them. The books are full of a mixture of political and religious enthusiasm, and dreamlike visions of the future that awaits Israel. They have their origin in the books of the ancient prophets and try to establish connections with them. The Book of Daniel, dating from Maccabean times, already resembles them, and like it they choose distinguished figures from the past as their mouthpieces. Enoch, Baruch, Ezra, and even the heathen Sibyl, give the books their titles.

The Messianic dreams were expounded in great detail.

God created not one, but two ages. The first was the present one and it could be viewed only with the most profound pessimism. The lord of this world was the devil and hostile renegade powers ruled the nations. But it aspired to the second age when God's power would gain the mastery. And when our age was ebbing out, its close would be marked by terrible birth pangs and struggles. The new world would be born in travail.

This is a field in which imagination has always given itself full rein. And the Messianic dream is no different from many others that have revelled in the terrors of our last days. Mankind would see a sword in the sky and the sun extinguished in mid course; wood would drip blood and stones begin to speak. But there would also be signs among men that the end of the world was near. Truth and loyalty would disappear; human bodies would wither and the great become small; children less than a year old would speak properly; women would give birth to monsters; fresh springs would yield salt water; sown fields would suddenly become as if left fallow and full store-rooms would be found empty.

But on the day when their need was greatest the Messiah would come. He would take his stand in the midst of Israel and when the enemy attacked he would annihilate them with the breath of his mouth. The wicked would be judged and Israel would govern the world with justice. Her rule would endure for a thousand years of happiness and would replenish the earth.

The Messianic visions have no kind of unity. The most heterogeneous elements are interwoven, from crassly materialistic expectations to deep intuitions with genuine glimpses of spirituality. There were not only enthusiastic and inflamed patriots, looking for him who was to free the nation from the Roman yoke; the old prophecies by Isaiah about the Suffering Servant of the Lord, bruised and wounded for our misdeeds, he who took our chastisement upon himself so that we might have peace, also belong to the picture. And there were men who dreamed of a mystical semi-divine

Messiah, who would redeem men from their sins. They
exhorted mankind to wait and hope—as in the famous passage from 2 Esdras iv, in which the author cannot restrain
his impatient longing for the Messiah, who is nowhere to be
seen, and God's answer:

'Do not thou hasten above the most Highest.'

The idea of the Messiah and his coming kingdom is
unique in Judaism and one of its gifts to mankind. The Greeks,
the Romans and many other ancient nations were also familiar
with a golden age. But in their case it belongs to the past
and was a lost world. Judaism dimly sees its golden age in
the future at the end of time. When the Messiah comes, evil
and all strife shall disappear, swords shall be turned into
ploughshares and the lion lie down with the lamb, the earth
shall be filled with knowledge of the Lord as water covers
the sea. The dispersed people will gather again in the land
of their fathers and David's kingdom be restored. But salvation applies to all mankind. The belief in the dawn behind
the blackest night, that the good, the true and the just have
the last word, is Jewish.

But the Jewish Messiah is a man. A great man, indeed
the greatest God has created. The words of the Psalm, 'Thou
hast made him a little lower than the angels', apply especially
to the Messiah. But the word 'lower' places him among men
and never allows the Messiah to cross this border. The Jewish kingdom is 'of this world'.

And that night when a woman in a stable behind an inn
in Bethlehem swaddled the child she had borne and the
angels sang Christmas in, the voice was first heard that thirty
years later spoke the words which decreed the difference:

'My kingdom is not of this world.'

JESUS WAS NOT A CHRISTIAN; HE WAS A JEW. The average churchgoer would get a shock if he heard those words from the pulpit. Jesus, God's only begotten son, the founder of Christianity, was not a Christian, but a Jew, he who must be called the first of the Christians!

If a Jew had uttered the words, no one would have been surprised. It goes without saying that Jews completely strip the figure of Jesus of all the church's adornments—divinity, the fact of redemption, resurrection from the dead, return as universal judge—and reduce the church's saviour to an ordinary Jew, a man who lived two thousand years ago and whom the Romen occupation forces in Judaea executed because he was suspected to be a troublemaker. Naturally there are Jews like Albert Einstein who can say that they are fascinated by the Nazarene's brilliant personality, and willingly include him in the ranks of great Jews. But the general attitude is 'on guard' and there are reasons for this.

In its dealings with the Christian church, Judaism has always been the underdog, which has claws without being able to retaliate. It cost the Jew dear to reply to Christian provocation. His silent answer was to shut himself in, lock the door, pull the curtains and live alone with his family in his own house. Later we shall follow the Jewish reaction to Jesus through the ages. But a typical example is provided by J. H. Hertz, the British chief rabbi who died only twenty years ago. He consistently avoided mentioning Jesus's name and merely called him 'the founder of Christianity'. But when it came to discussions between the two religions and open confrontation, it was obviously clever tactics for the Jews to claim Jesus as one of themselves. It was like the synagogue capturing Christianity's standard and setting it up in their own citadel.

Jesus was not a Christian; he was a Jew.

That is the Jewish view of Jesus, which has been handed down without change from generation to generation. Jesus was a Jew, a man. It is only Christianity which believes that he is the Messiah and God's only begotten son.

And yet it was *not* a Jew who formulated that challenging and oft-quoted sentence, but a Christian, a great Protestant theologian, Julius Wellhausen, who was one of the pioneers of modern biblical research a little less than a hundred years ago.

The words are carried to extremes; like all paradoxes they show only one facet of the truth to the light, so that it grips us and compels reflection. But when we talk of eternal truths, those on which life and death depend, and in which men dare to approach the riddle of the world, they are seldom covered by a single phrase. For Truth, written with a capital T, has many aspects and some of them may seem to contradict each other. This is where the paradox is useful, so long as people remember the defect inseparable from paradoxes, that by emphasising one facet of the truth they obscure others. Understood in this way, it is worth listening to Wellhausen, for he is quite right.

Jesus was in fact a Jew; he lived and died as a man of Israel. A modern Jewish historian like Joseph Klausner says of him: 'He was the most Jewish of Jews, even more Jewish than Hillel.' Both from the human and religious point of view Jesus's background was Judaism, as it was moulded by the best men among the people, i.e. the Pharisees. His sayings about the kingdom of God, men's relations with God and one another, are almost identical with the preaching of the Pharisees that modern research has brought to light.

G

Jesus's childhood was spent in Galilee, the patriots' strong-hold; he spoke Aramaic, the popular tongue, and was brought up on the Torah and the scriptures. The oral tradition and popular literature, the visions of the Apocrypha and the Pseudepigrapha, were also well known to him. Like other Jews he went to the synagogue on the Sabbath and said the prayer Shema every day: 'Hear, O Israel, the Lord our God is One.' When he healed a leper, he told him to show himself to the priest and make the offering that Moses had commanded. The rich young man asked what he should do to inherit eternal life and Jesus answered that he should obey the commandments. Three basic verses in the Sermon on the Mount run: 'Think not that I am come to destroy the law, or the prophets: I am come not to destroy, but to fulfil. For verily I say unto you, till heaven and earth pass, one jot or tittle shall in no wise pass from the law, till all be fulfilled. Whosoever, therefore, shall break one of these least commandments and shall teach men so, he shall be called the least in the kingdom of heaven.'

There could be no more unconditional expression of respect for the Torah. A casual utterance often says more than a lengthy disquisition. For example, this one in the parable of the rich man and Lazarus: 'If they hear not Moses and the prophets, neither will they be persuaded, though one rose from the dead.' The only non-Jew Jesus performed a miracle for was the woman of Canaan. Like all Jews he made a distinction between the heathens and himself and said to her: 'I am not sent but unto the lost sheep of the house of Israel', and when the woman persisted in her request, the normal Jewish expression of contempt came involuntarily to his lips; he compared the heathens to dogs. It is impossible for an oriental to say anything more disparaging about a person than that he is a dog. The same disdain is heard in his admonitions 'not to be as the heathens' and 'when ye pray, do not use vain repetitions as the heathens do'.

These examples are chosen at random to fill in the

picture of Christ as a Jew. The Bible reader will readily recognise them and be able to supplement them with others from the many examples in the Gospels. But it is enough to illustrate the assertion that Jesus was a Jew. And it is right to emphasise the original close relationship between Judaism and Christianity. For it is largely forgotten by the church. In its preaching the image of Jesus all too often disappears in a mass of pious generalisations and lacks the sharp outlines conferred by his Jewish origin. As always, he who forgets his childhood home and first beginnings is impoverished.

That is not the whole story. It is certainly a fact that Christianity emerged from Judaism and that its germ was Jewish. But it is just as clear a fact that Judaism never became Christianity and chose to go its own way. Voltaire says that the great contradiction is that even if Jesus was a Jew, those who followed him were not Jews. So right from the beginning there must have been a decisive difference between the two, and it should be possible to trace this divergence back to Jesus himself. And sure enough we do find it in him who did not come to put a piece of new cloth on an old garment or pour new wine into old bottles, he who dared to say: 'Ye have heard that it was said by them of old time . . . But I say unto you.'

Jesus was a Jew and yet he made a distinction between himself and his people.

Before we open the ancient books to look for all the available truth about Jesus and the break between him and Israel, we must realise that no religion reveals its innermost secrets to scholarly research. At one point or another the research-worker is forced to stop in humiliation and admit that rational and objective investigation will take him no further.

Of course, it is to be hoped that up to this point he has been able to draw attention to obviously false and empty doctrines and clear the ground of them. Modern biblical scholarship has done a useful job of weeding in both Old and New Testaments. When the Almighty revealed His intention to redeem us and had frail erring men write it down for future generations, He gave us the treasure in clay vessels, so to speak. The precious metal remains unharmed if the clay is taken to pieces and examined. Perhaps damage is done to prejudices and 'inherited truths', but honest courageous research must follow the paths indicated by considered thinking. Both brains and a tireless urge to force their way through the mist that conceals those distant ages are the equipment that the Creator supplied men with. It is his intention that we should use them.

But only so far as they can be used. For there are domains where scholarly proofs and counterproofs are meaningless, because they are beyond the scope of thought. The personality of Jesus is one of them.

Jesus is the Messiah, the Son of God.

The Jew says 'no' to this assertion and the Christian says 'yes'. But both answers are creeds. The Jew cannot say 'yes' without ceasing to be a Jew, but he simply cannot prove that his 'no' is the right answer. The Christian is equally incapable of proving his 'yes' correct, in the same way that a law of nature or a mathematical formula is left open, and only the blind or foolish deny it. In the last instance both Judaism and Christianity depend on a personal choice, something that is beyond proof, namely conviction. The Gospel according to St. John attributes to Jesus some wise words that say the same thing: 'If any man will do His will, he shall know of the doctrine, whether it be of God, or whether I speak it of myself.' I may also quote Martin Buber: 'No man outside Israel knows Israel's secret. And no one outside Christianity knows Christianity's secret. But without knowing, each can recognise the other.'

The literature about the Gospels and their picture of Jesus fills libraries. It is so vast that its study is a discipline in itself. It is estimated that more than 60,000 books have been written about Jesus. Eight hundred languages and dialects tell his story. The most varied theories about the Gospels' value have been put forward. From the heavy-handed inspirational attitude that every word was inspired by God they pass through every conceivable shade of opinion to end in the far-fetched hypothesis that Jesus was a mystical figure who never existed except in legend. In his old age Georg Brandes accepted the last proposition, regardless of the fact that the tradition of Jesus rests on far firmer foundations than our knowledge of Socrates, whose existence no one doubts.

I should never stop if I enumerated everything that imaginative scholars have found in Jesus. They have mostly seen an image of their own ideals and dreams. Jesus was the first socialist; Tolstoy saw him as his predecessor in threatening the established state and the community. Others made him a philosopher reminiscent of modern liberal politicians, not to mention the German antisemites who turned him into a blond and blue-eyed Aryan who abhorred Jews.

A sober evaluation, and there is broad agreement about it, accepts the Gospel stories on the whole, but naturally puts a question mark after some details and ascribes different values to the source materials behind them. We must not imagine that the four Gospels were written all ready for consumption, that they were suddenly on the book market and the church possessed the beginning of the New Testament. Admittedly the Gospels come first in the New Testament, but they are not the oldest stratum in it. Paul's epistles are older. It is also useful to remember that it was not the Gospels which created the church, but on the contrary the church which wrote the Gospels; the church existed before they did. Nor were they written in the form that we know, for they are the record of a development within the budding church. We can even read ecclesiastical history in them; they involuntarily mirror the views of changing times and give an insight into them. It is of secondary importance whether the authors of the Gospels are really the four men whose names they bear. In olden times it was the custom to put the names of well-known men on books to which it was desired to attract attention. The main thing is the value and credibility of their contents.

The Gospels began as stories that went from mouth to mouth. We have already seen that the Jews were brought up to listen and remember. And no one paid stricter attention than the disciples to every word from Jesus's lips. They were indelibly stamped on their memories and were repeated and discussed over and over again. Parts of the tradition were written down at an early date; it is taken for granted that at least some passages of the Gospels are based on written sources. Nevertheless, it was unavoidable that the stories circulated in varying forms, which resulted in discrepancies and contradictions. The translation into Greek also hides the original tone that the Aramaic vernacular had given them.

But the Gospels, in the form that we have them in the New Testament, can stand being put under the microscope of criticism. There is about them a genuine flavour of Palestine in the first century of our era as we know the country and people from other sources, and the topographical knowledge they display is very accurate. Moreover, the background to daily life, as seen in customs and holidays and faith, is so naturally correct that we can safely assume that the description of Jesus and his surroundings stems from eye-witnesses, whether they were the men who wrote the Gospels as we know them, or later authors whose names are unknown to us. But the Gospels are not biographies or historiography in the modern sense of the word. Their purpose is religious; each of the four authors gives his own account of Jesus as the man the prophets had foretold would come to set Israel free.

No one can help noticing the difference between the first three Gospels on the one hand, and the fourth on the other. The last, traditionally ascribed to the apostle John, 'the disciple, whom the Lord loved', is the latest of all the Gospels, probably written about the year 100. In other words, it represents a late phase in Christianity's early development.

It has high value as literature; the picture of Jesus, simplified, dreaming and remote from reality, emerges from its pages almost like an abstraction. The author was obviously influenced by his familiarity with Philo's ideas.

The first three Gospels stand in close relationship to each other and partly stem from the same sources. Even though they are stamped by the different personalities of their authors, the books are so alike that they are sometimes printed side by side in parallel columns to facilitate comparison. This is called a synopsis and they are in fact known as the Synoptic Gospels. The Gospel according to St. Mark, written some years before the destruction of Jerusalem, is considered to be the oldest of them. Then comes St. Luke's Gospel from some time in the 70's and the latest is St. Matthew's Gospel. Once we have grasped this we are equipped to investigate what the Gospels say about the beginnings of the break between Jesus and the people's teachers and the far-reaching consequences that resulted.

The first thing we study is how the Gospels unconsciously tell the church's history, often between the lines and in chance sentences. The gulf between the young church and the synagogue opened and became visible soon after Jerusalem's destruction, but grew rapidly wider as the Church's development continued. And through the Gospels we catch glimpses of the widening process. In the late Gospel according to St. John the church's dislike of the synagogue has increased so much that the word 'Jews' is automatically used in a hostile sense and indicates those who are against Jesus. Here all Jews are lumped together. Priests and Pharisees are in close alliance against Jesus, and everything evil comes from them. The split is a fact about which it is superfluous to argue. If St. John's Gospel had been our only source, I think hardly anyone would have believed that Jesus and the disciples were Jews, so synonymous are Jews and hostility. But in the Synoptists the observant reader finds a growing and gradual deterioration of Jesus's relations with his fellow-countrymen. So they are the texts we examine closely in order to look for the crack which finally became a gulf.

Small details catch our attention first. We notice one of them if we set the three accounts of John the Baptist side by side. Mark refers to the Baptist's preaching of the baptism of repentance for the remission of sins in a few words, but Luke and Matthew give details. From them we know that the passionate revivalist cried: 'O generation of vipers, who hath warned you to flee from the wrath to come?' In Luke the words are directed at 'the multitude that came forth to be baptised of him', but Matthew makes them explode when 'he saw many of the Pharisees and Sadducees come'. In other words, Mark is neutral, nor does the later Luke exaggerate, while Matthew, the last of the three, takes sides against the Jewish authorities.

The account of the man sick of the palsy whom Jesus heals reflects the same attitude. This is all the more remarkable because here all three Synoptists draw on the same written source. An identical sudden transition to direct speech shows this; every reader has been startled by it. It is found in the middle of the story where Jesus forgives the sick man his sins. This angers the scribes who witnessed the event. But here we see the difference. Mark and Luke make Jesus answer: 'Why reason ye these things in your hearts?', but Matthew has: 'Wherefore think ye *evil* in your hearts?' Admittedly these are minor details, but they are found throughout the Gospels and reflect a tendency.

All three Synoptists tell us about the attention Jesus attracted by his preaching and his miracles, and that great crowds followed him. Soon both religious and political authorities kept him under surveillance. But it was surprisingly long before anyone intervened. His teaching was quite in keeping with that of the Pharisees. Naturally enough it offended them that he associated 'with publicans and sinners', i.e. men who did not observe the strict rules of the Pharisees, but there were so many schools in the Judaism of the time that it cannot be called provocative hostility. On many occasions the Pharisees discussed such episodes, but they did not result in a break.

But the crisis between Jesus and the Pharisees had to come. The reason seems slender enough to us, but it disclosed so deep a difference between the two parties that it became disastrous. Here we see the beginning of the break. It happened like this.

One Sabbath Jesus's disciples were hungry. They picked some ears of corn and ate them. This was harvesting, forbidden by tradition on the Sabbath, and the Pharisees criticised Jesus violently for allowing it. It shocked them that the new teacher treated established customs so casually. And not long after he did something similar. Jesus met a man with a withered hand in the synagogue. According to tradition it was only permissible to practise medicine on the Sabbath if a life was in imminent danger, and a withered hand is not an acute illness. So when Jesus healed the man it was an open challenge to the Pharisees. With this action he threw down the gauntlet at their feet. From that moment they were enemies; no other party among the Jews opposed him as much as the Pharisees. We read in Matthew that they 'held a council against him, how they might destroy him'. This should not be taken literally, but it is an example of this evangelist's dislike of the Jews. There are no reports that the Pharisees took part in the lawsuit against Jesus.

During the sharp clash on that day Jesus uttered words which Mark has preserved as 'The sabbath was made for man, and not man for the sabbath', while Matthew has 'For the Son of man is Lord even of the sabbath day'. Properly understood, the first sentence could not create a dispute; it is found in almost the same form in the Pharisees' teaching. Nevertheless, the assertion, especially together with the sentence in Matthew, opens our eyes to the reason for the conflict between Jesus and the Pharisees. It sprang from the two parties' widely differing views of God's will and man's relation to it. The fact that the climax came when Jesus

broke the law of the Sabbath, or more accurately the Pharisees' interpretation of it, was a coincidence. They could just
as well have clashed over other points. The dispute was not
about details but about principles.

It was never the question of obedience to the Torah that
separated Jesus from the Pharisees. We have already seen
that Jesus honoured the Torah and taught others to follow
its commandments. This tallies with the fact that we search
the gospels in vain for criticism by the Pharisees of Jesus's
teaching about the Kingdom of Heaven, sin, prayer, penance and forgiveness. In all these fields Jesus was as good a
Jew as any Pharisee. Even the Gospel according to St. John
makes him say 'For salvation is of the Jews', and on one occasion it was the Pharisees who warned Jesus that his life was in
danger.

When the dispute about the Sabbath flared up, it was
not because Jesus disregarded the actual commandment. Yet
the Sabbath was perhaps the Jews' most precious possession.
In olden times they were the only people that kept a weekly
holiday. The Sabbath, more than anything else, marked the
barrier between Jew and heathen. Therefore the Pharisees
guarded it and surrounded it with carefully devised, detailed
ordinances, which they wanted observed to the letter.

It is easy enough to smile at the blatant pedantry
exhibited by Judaism with its finicky solicitude for keeping
the Sabbath undefiled. And the church authorities did smirk
when they patronisingly quoted some of the Pharisaic rules.
For example: the Jew must not carry burdens on the Sabbath. A burden is painstakingly defined as anything heavier
than a dried fig, and it is even debated whether it is permissible to use one's false teeth on the Sabbath. Nor can fire
be lit or put out, and in the long lists of what this implies
we read that the Jew may put a bowl under a burning oil-
lamp but that there must be no water in the bowl, for there
is a risk of burning oil dripping into it and that is putting
fire out. Not to mention harvesting on the Sabbath, when it
is forbidden to pluck a blade of grass or remove withered

leaves. These endless regulations are like stones in the wall
that protects the Sabbath. Naturally others, who have not
lived inside it since childhood, think that the wall is built
too high and that there are far too many small stones in it.
But it *is* a wall, and generation after generation have helped
in its building. Why be amused by evidence of the watch
kept by a scrupulously sensitive conscience to see that man
walked correctly according to God's will? Behind it all lies a
vital principle. And it was this that Jesus twice broke with
on the Sabbath. His vital principle was diametrically opposed
to the Pharisees'.

But if this is correct, it sounds reasonable when the
traditional Christian explanation of the break between Jesus
and the Pharisees says that Jesus did observe the written
Torah, but rejected the oral law, that he went back to the
prophets of Israel, whereas the Pharisees represented the
study of the law, which had replaced the prophets and was
coming into foul, stagnant water. Here were the Pharisees
fussing and bothering about formalities and quibbles, while
Jesus raised the major issues and vital standpoints. Once
again the usual caricature of the Pharisees is refurbished and
exposed to general contempt.

However, we have already seen that this portrait of the
Pharisees does not correspond to reality and is only perpetu-
ated by ignorance. But it is also superficial to dismiss such
a profound break as the one we are witness to with a cheap
commentary. We must go deeper and discover the difference
in the two attitudes to life that lay behind the adherence of
both Jesus and the Pharisees to their particular point of view.

One of Jesus's loveliest parables illustrates what we are
talking about here—the parable of the man who seeks and
finds a pearl of great price and sells everything he possesses
so that the pearl may be his. The parable is saying that there
is something in the world, one single thing, that is so great
and so lofty that everything else becomes as nothing compared with it. And Jesus knew himself to be so regally free in
his communion with the Father that he could point to this

Lincoln Christian College

unique thing. The kingdom of heaven is at hand; seek it and everything else will be given as well. This he taught as one having authority and not as the scribes.

That is the difference between the two sides. Jesus did not feel himself bound by what others had said, but advanced alone with intuitive assurance, to use an expression from modern psychology, to the heart of the matter. It was inevitable that he should sweep many traditional sections of the law to one side. Not because he opposed them, but because he hardly noticed them. They did not exist for him.

Let us return to the Sabbath. Jesus looked on it as a day of rest. But it was artificial and unnatural to forbid the gathering of a handful of corn or the healing of a sick man on this day of rest. After all, the Sabbath was made for man. In this way he rejected the outworks, or more accurately he did not see them and bypassed them to attack the fortress's central tower. He could do so, because he stood in such a confidential filial relationship to the All Highest that the kingdom of heaven came with him.

The Pharisees went the opposite way. They never rejected the old because it was old. Like faithful householders they guarded what their fathers had handed down to them. They laid new and old, the important and the less important on top of one another. Every single thing was of value, however slight it was. Piled up, these things built the wall behind which the people could live and serve God.

The fact is that the Pharisees were the heirs of Ezra's reformation. Neither he nor they aimed at creating a new Jewish religion to replace that of the prophets. On the contrary, their laborious task was to weave the prophets' teaching into everyone's daily life. They succeeded in this; they raised the people far above the level they had reached in the days of the prophets. The prophets, both major and minor, had fought desperately against idolatry in Israel, with poor results. But in the whole of the New Testament there is not one mention of idolatry among the Jews at the time I am writing about, in spite of all the temptations the heathens enticed them with. The Pharisees' methods did reach one goal, but they were still on their way to others. In a difficult time that was full of problems, they stood at the centre of a development whose continuing existence they had to fight for every day. Naturally they viewed with anxiety a teacher who acted directly contrary to their time-honoured experiences.

The Pharisees' goal was to lead the people, the whole people, to God and to keep them with Him with the help of a tested system. Every single action every day and throughout their lives was to remind them of the Almighty and follow the spirit of His teaching. But Jesus led men, one by one, straight to the Father. Everything he considered superfluous was swept to one side. In his eyes the Pharisees were *almost* right. But this 'almost' turned their right into wrong, so true it is that the next best is the best's worst enemy. The prevailing Christian explanation that the Pharisees were blind and one hundred per cent wrong can be forgotten; it is too cheap. The conflict was between two parties, each of which was right, working from its own assumptions. It is a dilemma of this kind that creates tragedy.

Both parties had their roots in the same religion. We usually call them mother and daughter. It would be more accurate to see them as elder and younger sisters. For, all things considered, Judaism is not the forerunner of Christianity. Both grew up side by side in the same soil, but afterwards their ways parted.

And if communion with God can be recognised by peace of mind in life and death, two thousand years' experience tells us that both ways are made by God and lead to the goal.

'Art thou he that should come? or look we for another?'

Longing, uncertainty and growing disappointment vibrate in the question John the Baptist sent to Jesus from prison. For Jesus was quite different from the Messiah John and the whole of Israel had waited for.

Expectation of the Messiah and the new age that was

to come with him made Israel like a volcano on the verge of eruption. Every day one section or another of the subjugated people was wrought up to a feverish and exalted state of excitement in which anything could happen.

And now Jesus was the focus of attention. Rumours about the new teacher went from village to village: the remarkable power in him that healed the sick and called the dead from the grave, the visions in his words and the kingdom of heaven that was at hand. But never the inflammatory appeal to dig up hidden weapons and go to war against the hated Roman soldiers. Their snarling shouts of command and the ring of their iron-studded shoes trampling over Jewish earth were supposed to be silenced by the Messiah. But no, the Jesus they saw was a Messiah singled out not for conquest, victory and power, but for service, suffering and death.

For God's thoughts are not men's thoughts. Reality, as God shapes it, seldom corresponds to man's dreams of what it should be. That is a bitter truth that the nations of the earth have continually experienced. And no people so often as the chosen one. When God in olden times led his people out of the Egyptian bondage with his mighty hand, when he shattered Pharaoh's defiance and opened the way through the Red Sea, everyone expected a swift victorious advance into the promised land. But no, there were endless decades of wandering in a wilderness which made the Israelites long to return to the fleshpots of Egypt. We have hindsight and see that in just this way God prepared his people to receive the Torah at Sinai. But he who has to learn that God never hurries and that His plans are higher than men can conceive, must struggle through doubt before he is able to bow to God's will and see His greatness.

And just as the revelation on Golgotha corresponds to God's words from Sinai, the people in Jesus's day experienced the same doubt that their fathers once became bogged down in. The old prophetic books were brought out and studied; devout men wondered whether Jesus was really the man who had been foretold. It was not easy to decide, for the prophets only spoke of the person of the Messiah in obscure language. Significantly enough, Matthew, who tries to represent Jesus's life and work as that which is 'spoken by the prophets', gives only insignificant and anecdotal details as proofs. For example, he says that Jesus rode on an ass, that he spoke in parables and praised the children in the temple.

The fact is that although the prophets were vague in their descriptions of Messiah the man, they spoke in much more colourful and clearer words about the new age he was to usher in. And here doubt stared blankly, for where was the golden age with peace and harmony and Jerusalem as queen of the earth? Everything went on in the same depressing way as before.

So much the stronger was the effect of Jesus's confident certainty that he was the man who should come. St. John's Gospel tells us that he proclaimed it right at the beginning of his ministry, in his dealings with Nicodemus and the woman of Samaria. The Synoptists are surely more accurate when they described his conviction as growing quietly and being hid for a long time. Jesus rejoiced in Peter's confession, but forbade public homage. When an enthusiastic crowd wanted to proclaim him king, he withdrew and hid himself. He only allowed a public proclamation during the last days of his life, when he entered Jerusalem on Palm Sunday. The event was exploited by his enemies; it was the basis for the accusation that led him to the cross.

No prophet had predicted that the Messiah would be rejected by his own people and die a felon's death. Not until the terrible thing happened and the brutal reality was disclosed on a bloody cross, was light thrown on Isaiah's obscure words about the Suffering Servant of the Lord. The prophet did not have a specific person in mind; to him the people was the Lord's Servant. But the image fitted Jesus' agony and death; the words became classical when describing them. Only then did prophecy and reality join hands. As this dawned upon people, the church was already on a road that led far away from Judaism.

'His blood be upon us, and on our children.'

That quotation comes from the Gospel according to St. Matthew and refers to the cry on Good Friday. In other words, it is from the latest of the Synoptic Gospels, written at a time when tension between church and synagogue was growing. So the author found it natural to paint the Jews' share in Jesus's death as blackly as possible. The fact that he did so was disastrous. An echo of that cry has reverberated down the ages and has never been forgotten by the church. From it grew, like a hideous rampant weed, the accusation that the Jews were deicides, and countless Jews have suffered for it. People forgot that Jesus said on the cross: 'Father, forgive them; for they know not what they do', and no one seems to have realised that an accidentally assembled crowd could never represent the millions of Jewish people in Palestine and throughout the world, still less unborn generations.

When Jesus was seized in the Garden of Gethsemane, his friends fled and none of them was present at his trial behind the closed doors of the palace. So we should not be surprised to find that there are many discrepancies in the Gospels about this particular incident. When laymen give an account of a complicated case at which they have not been present, such discrepancies are unavoidable. But since the problem of responsibility for Jesus's conviction has cast long shadows over relations between the two religions, we can well understand that modern Jews reject the idea that the case ought to be revived and its details reconstructed. Yet it might succeed once and for all in driving a stake through the hideous spectre that the accusation of deicide has been. But even without a new lawsuit, it is possible, at least in broad outline, to reconstruct the course of events during the twelve hours which acquired eternal importance for mankind.

Jesus went to Jerusalem at Passover to meet the great men and challenge them. Until then he had worked among the common people and shown men the way to God and proclaimed His kingdom. Jesus knew that he came from God in a unique way and was to create something new. But in the early stages of his mission he had still only managed to sow his words among the few. It still remained to wrestle with the community, with the State, and ask for the doors to be opened to his message, whether it pleased the great ones or not. That the road would be bloody and that his death was a link in the Almighty's plan, he had long guessed and talked about to his friends.

So he made his entry into Jerusalem and let the masses pay homage to him. They looked on him as the king who enters a conquered city. On that one day he was the man foretold, he who should come. In our time palms are a symbol of peace, but in antiquity they signified the victorious conqueror. When people threw palm branches in Jesus's path, it meant that henceforth he would tread the oppressors underfoot. And in the temple he attracted public attention when he rid the forecourts of moneychangers and trades-men.

All at once the prophet from remote provincial towns had become a national figure in the capital, just as it was full to overflowing with Passover visitors from near and far. This was what made the authorities nervous. Not his proclama-tion. It made no impression on them, particularly because they knew that the Romans attached no importance to religious disputes in conquered countries. But it was quite conceivable that the Romans might suspect that a man who let himself be acclaimed and who rid the temple of booths might also cherish plans for ridding the country of the Roman eagles.

The high priest and the circle around him would have done anything to preserve the slender remnants of self-government the Romans still granted them. The problem was simply how they could render Jesus harmless without

H

losing their own popularity with everyone who admired him.

So they decided to seize Jesus secretly by night. They did not bring him before the great religious council, the Sanhedrin, but before the high priest's own more intimate council, an institution that the Romans not only tolerated but also encouraged vassal states to set up, so as to have available a local authority with which they could negotiate. This council was composed of the high priest's closest collaborators, namely the Sadducees. Here we have the explanation why the Pharisees were not involved in the conviction of Jesus, which they would probably have protested against. Even though they were in complete disagreement with him, they did not want him condemned to death.

But the council acted quickly and effectively: two nocturnal meetings for a hearing and judgment, then the handing over of the condemned man to the Romans, when Pilate in vain tried to put the responsibility on others but finally allowed the sentence to be carried out. The whole thing took place in twelve hours.

Thus the question of Jesus's conviction can be settled by saying that political, not religious considerations, made the Jewish authorities judge Jesus and hand him over to the Romans. It is an established fact that the latter carried out the execution. The Jewish punishment for blasphemy was stoning. Crucifixion was a Roman punishment used for traitors and rebels. The inscription that Pilate had placed on the cross, that Jesus was king of the Jews, is evidence that the Romans considered him as a rebel.

The church has symbolised the dead Christ by the Paschal lamb. But the true symbol should not be sought there; it lies in the ritual for the Day of Atonement and the sacrifice of the scapegoat. Yet no symbol is adequate to interpret Jesus's submission to God's will even to the shameful death on the cross, or what the Almighty intended by it. We stand in silence before the mystery. Either we bow to the cross or we avoid it.

One thing is certain, that Christianity would have been

as empty without the cross as Judaism without the Torah.

But the heart of the growing church's faith in the first few decades after Golgotha was not the cross, but Jesus's resurrection. Paul was the first man to ponder deeply over the riddle of the cross and try to throw light on it.

HE IS RISEN.

To his friends the vision of Jesus's triumph over his terrible crucifixion shone like sunrise after a pitch-black night. In a flash the doubt and despair of the first disciples was swept aside. The Christian church raised its spire to heaven above the ruins of their shattered faith. The resurrection of Jesus was then and is today the firm foundation on which the Christian faith rests, undemonstrable intellectually, but a part of what we saw Martin Buber call Christianity's secret.

There was still to be a long process of development before the rift between the growing church and the synagogue became visible to everybody. Judaism in those days was a broad concept. It contained a wealth of nuances, and the church was provisionally considered as one of its many sects. Jesus's disciples were still Jews in Jerusalem and they took part in the temple services. Some of them were Pharisees, the majority ignorant people; some, who spoke Aramaic, were born in Judaea itself, others were so-called Hellenistic Jews, Greek speakers from other countries, but settled in Jerusalem where Jews and proselytes from different nations had their own synagogues. The only difference between these Nazarenes, as they were called, and other Jews was that they recognized the name of the Messiah, the resurrected Jesus, who would soon return triumphantly as victor and judge. The basic source of our knowledge of those early days is the Acts of the Apostles or *Acta*, the Latin for actions, as the book is sometimes called. Most scholars agree that the author was the Gentile Christian and Greek doctor Luke. Paul met him on one of his journeys; he was baptised and followed the apostles for long periods. In the Gospel according to St. Luke, which is also written by him, we read about his methods of collecting material. Luke sought out eyewitnesses and carefully examined everything before he wrote. His books set a high standard, both as literature and for objectivity. When he repeats conversations, they are of course reconstructed, but it is impressive to see how, in his reports of words that were spoken thirty or forty years before he himself wrote, he avoids the temptation of phrasing them in the preaching style of his own day. It increases our respect for him as a writer.

Simon Peter was a dominant figure in the church's early years. Every new movement needs a leader of his type in its first critical phase. We are well aware that Peter had a changeable temperament, now blazing fiercely, now doubtful and uncertain—indeed, he once denied his master. He possessed neither the culture and scholarship of St. Paul nor his perseverance and tactical ability. Nevertheless, the simple fisherman from Galilee was a warm-hearted and enthusiastic believer with vision and imagination. The experience of his encounter with Christ risen from the dead had convinced him and conquered his weaknesses. Confronted with hostile authorities, he was courageous and unshakeable in his testimony. That is how he earned his nickname of Cephas, the Rock.

Jesus's brother, James, stood by Peter's side. Tradition describes him almost as an Essene. James did not drink wine or eat meat. He let his hair and beard grow, and wore a linen robe, never woollen clothes. He was called the Just. Visitors to the temple saw him kneeling and praying for the remission of the people's sins. He prayed so often and so long that his knees became as hardened as a camel's.

The first congregation in Jerusalem appears in a transfigured light to later generations. It observed the teaching of the apostles, the breaking of bread and the prayers. Its adherents went every day to the sanctuary and broke bread at home. They received their food with gladness and singleness of heart, for they praised God and were favoured among all people. And the Lord daily supplied souls who wanted to be saved. That is how the Acts' description of the church sounds literally. And Acts adds that they had everything in common. This form of voluntary communism shows that they wanted to be brothers and sisters, without distinction between rich and poor. It was actually possible for them to put this into practice because they knew that the end was near. Soon God's kingdom would come with the return of Jesus. So why let oneself be bound by Mammon? It was inevitable that such a fellowship should be attractive to others.

The idyll did not last long. When Peter healed a lame man, the Nazarenes came into the searchlight of publicity. The temple authorities intervened and Peter was frequently accused before the courts. It is significant that in his first speeches he tried to modify the Jews' responsibility for the death of Jesus; the fact that Jesus was executed by lawless hands took place with God's firm intention and foreknowledge. A decisive break was averted by the highly esteemed Pharisee Gamaliel, who said something that will always be valid about tolerance and the truth that continues to exist when ideas that are not what they pretend to be gain currency: 'If this counsel or this work be of men, it will come to nought: But if it be of God, ye cannot overthrow it.'

But events came to a head when an overheated mob stoned Stephen. He had discussed the new faith with other Hellenistic Jews. They came from far away and were used to front-line service for the Jewish faith. So they were annoyed by the Nazarenes' proclamation of a crucified Messiah and hurled themselves into a debate with the eager recently-converted Stephen. It ended in a lawsuit. In the middle of it, frenzied spectators threw themselves on the accused, carried him away and stoned him. The result was increased pressure on the Nazarenes and many of them fled for their lives. Only men like James were left in peace in the restless turbulent capital. The refugees scattered throughout the country and across its frontiers.

Once again it turned out that persecution and martyrdom always produce the opposite result from what they aim at. Far away from Jerusalem, in Samaria and Caesarea, even on the open highway near Gaza, the disciples had an opportunity to testify to the resurrected Christ and win new believers. And suddenly the young church saw itself faced with problems it was not ready to meet. For there were Gentiles, as well as Jews, among the new converts who accepted the gospel about Jesus. Peter baptised the centurion Cornelius in Caesarea. After much consideration, the leaders in Jerusalem approved his action. But neither Peter nor they realised the significance of opening the church's doors to the Gentiles.

The furthest place the message reached at this time was the capital of Syria, Antioch, the third largest city in the Roman Empire. There we hear for the first time of a systematic mission among the Gentiles, who joined the Christian church in large numbers. The word Christian can be applied to the church from this period; the name was coined in Antioch. On hearing rumours of events there, Jerusalem sent a reliable man, Barnabas, to investigate what was happening on the spot. He sent favourable reports home and travelled on to Tarsus to fetch Paul to help with the new congregation.

With Paul's name we come to a turning-point. The zealous young Pharisee Saul, as he was then called, was one of those who exchanged bitter words with Stephen. He stood guard over the clothes of the men who stoned the martyr and 'was consenting unto his death'. The same Saul was sent to Damascus by the council to wipe out the new heresy there. On his way he was suddenly converted by a vision to the Jesus he had persecuted. And the Jews had to watch their own plenipotentiary openly go over to the sect he was on his way to extirpate.

But before we deal with Saul who became Paul, let us

take a look at the wider world he came from and where his
ministry was to take place, the ministry which definitively
created the distinction between synagogue and church.

'For Moses of old time hath in every city them that
preach him, being read in the synagogues every sabbath day.'
We hear James the Just speaking those words in the Acts of
the Apostles. There are many other places in the old and
New Testaments which show us that the Jewish diaspora
covered the whole of the known world and had done so from
time immemorial, and every other source confirms this information. We have already made our acquaintance with
the great Jewish colonies in Babylon and Egypt. Soon Jews
also settled in Asia Minor and Greece. Pompey brought
prisoners from Jerusalem to Rome where they lived in big
Jewish settlements; their descendants are still to be found
in the old city. Wars and disturbances drove the Jews away
from their home country; others travelled voluntarily and
made themselves a future abroad. Most of them made a
success of it and achieved good living conditions. Contrary
to the custom at home, many of them became tradesmen.

Strong bonds linked the diaspora with Jerusalem. The
temple authorities always felt themselves lords of the vast
widespread Jewish people. And those abroad came to the holy
city on pilgrimages and sacrificed in the temple. It was a firm
rule that every Jew, wherever he lived, paid his half shekel
a year towards the maintenance of the temple. Altogether
this amounted to enormous sums that often tempted the
cupidity of those in power.

But it is an old experience that men who are uprooted
from their homeland seldom manage to settle abroad. There
is something rootless about their lives. And this was so of the
Jews in diaspora in olden times. The temptation to assimilation was obvious and many let themselves be tempted. They
forgot the holy language and knew the Bible only through
the Septuagint's Greek translation. They gave their children
Greek names. Jewish gravestones with Greek inscriptions are

found in many places and Jewish literature often betrays evidence of heathen influence. A diluted Judaism is weak. Even though the great majority steadily clung to their inherited faith with its customs and commandments, Paul met Jews everywhere who were ready to give up the old faith for the new one he brought.

A proselyte means one who has come over, i.e. to something else. The word has become naturalised in many languages as meaning a person who has gone over to Judaism. In our day Judaism holds itself proudly aloof and does not try to make proselytes. But when Christianity was on the point of becoming a universal religion, the Jews were zealous missionaries and won many proselytes. In the Gospel according to St. Matthew we read that the Pharisees willingly travelled by land and sea to make a single proselyte. And it was among proselytes at various stages that Paul harvested many new members for the church.

The proselyte was valued in Judaism. It was said that God loved him and wanted His people to bid the proselyte welcome and make him feel at home. It is a trend we find in ancient Judaism. One of the Talmud's legends tells us about it:

'A king had a flock of goats which were driven out to pasture every morning and brought home in the evening. Once a deer joined the goats and grazed with them and went into the fold with them every evening. The herdsman did not know what to do with it and asked the king for advice. He rejoiced over the deer and ordered them to give it pasture and water. In amazement they said to the king:

' "You own so many kids and goats that you take no notice of. But you look after the deer and give us orders about it."

'The king answered:

' "The goats have no choice. It is their nature to go to men's fields and find food and sleep in the fold at night. But deer belong to the wild world of nature; they are not made to live among us. Then shall we not rejoice over this one deer's leaving his fellows and coming to us?"'

And the parable continues:

'In the same way we must be thankful for the proselyte who leaves everything that was his and chooses to come to us.' And the Lord God ends the story with the words: 'Ye shall love and protect the proselyte more than your own.'

The parable is strikingly reminiscent of the one Jesus told about the shepherd who left the ninety-nine sheep that were in safety for the one that had gone astray and searched until he found it.

There were many proselytes. It is estimated that three million Jews lived in Palestine in Christ's day, with three and a half million outside the country, the latter figure excluding the Jews in Babylon, who lived outside the Roman Empire. But we realise that the Jews formed a sizeable minority in the Roman Empire. The great number of Jews in the diaspora could not possibly all have been the result of emigration from Palestine, but show how many proselytes there were. This tallies with evidence from other quarters. Roman authors such as Seneca and Dio Cassius refer to them. Horace mentions a friend who observes Jewish customs, 'like so many others'. A hostile witness, Tacitus complains that 'All kinds of dregs and homeless wretches flock to Jerusalem by the score'. Even a royal house went over to Judaism. Ananias, who was a merchant from Judaea, came to Adiabene, one of the vassal states of the Parthian Empire. There he won over the queen and the king's mother to his faith, and later King Izates and his sons followed suit. It is characteristic that the women were the first to be converted; everywhere it was the female sex who felt attracted by Judaism's lofty morality and emotional religion. When a pogrom was planned once in Damascus, none of the heathens dared initiate his wife into the plot. The women would betray it, for they all secretly belonged to Judaism.

But secret Jews of the kind the heathens dared not rely on were no rarity. They could be found at the foot of the imperial throne itself; Nero's queen, Poppaea Sabina, was one of them. We also hear of distinguished senators who sympathised with Israel's faith. They were called 'the god-fearing' and are often mentioned in the Acts of the Apostles —the Ethiopian queen's eunuch, whom Philip met on the way to Gaza, the centurion Cornelius Caesarea and Lydia, the seller of purple, in Philippi, to name some examples. To many heathens there was something fascinating about Judaism, its lofty monotheism and the Torah, which they could read in the Septuagint. Many of them admired Jewish customs such as the lighting of lamps on the Sabbath. The god-fearing went to the synagogues; they read the holy books. They were not Jews, but men still on the road, fumbling their way to an unknown God and the salvation they thirsted for, but did not find in heathendom.

Judaism throughout the Roman Empire, from rootless Jews and proselytes to the god-fearing, was like a field that was ready for harvest by a new religion that was built on Israel, but also offered something new. And the harvester came when Paul travelled round the enormous empire preaching the Gospel of Christ crucified and risen from the dead.

HE WAS SMALL OF STATURE, WITH CROOKED
legs and eyebrows that met over his nose; in
addition he was bald and had an aquiline pro-
truding nose. That is how people remember the apostle Paul,
who was obviously not the ideal man to take part in a beauty
contest. We also know that this ugly body was early marked
by abnormal exertions and injuries. Paul travelled halfway
round the world under primitive conditions. Many times he
was close to death, imprisoned, tried, whipped and mobbed.
On top of that, he was tormented by a physical infirmity. He
called it a thorn in the flesh, but it was probably the type of
epilepsy the ancients called the falling sickness. It is not
pleasant to see anyone have an attack of it, but a strikingly
large number of history's great figures, both religious and
secular, have been victims of epilepsy. However, the description of the great apostle does not end with these far from
flattering details. It is added that he radiated charm and that
his face could suddenly resemble an angel's countenance. It
must have been his eyes, with their vivid look, shining with
goodness or excitement at the greatness of what he was thinking or saying. We must imagine Paul standing in front of an
attentive meeting, or sitting with an individual, talking,
gesticulating and arguing as we see Jews do to this day,
while he developed and defended his opinions and tried to
win the others over to his side.

Paul was a man of contrasts. Like his physical make-up,

which was at the same time pitiful and captivating, his personality was full of opposing forces. But it is just such characters, composed of good and bad, high and low, always having to struggle against inner discords, who create true greatness. Shallow limited natures are all too often insipid and colourless. They seldom leave footsteps behind them that others burn to follow in.

Paul felt evil forces erupt inside him. There is more than rhetoric in expressions such as 'O wretched man that I am! Who shall deliver me from the body of this death?' or 'For the good that I would I do not: but the evil which I would not, that I do'. And if the task he was working on went wrong, he sank into melancholy and depression: 'And I was with you in weakness, and in fear, and in much trembling.' He took a dark, pessimistic view of the world and expected imminent catastrophe. His modern dread of annihilation makes him remarkably up to date. In his visions the whole creation sighs and is in childbirth, but in the same breath he proclaims the joyful war for victory over death and angels and powers, the present and the future, the deep and the lofty.

In his way Paul fits the saying that purity of heart is to desire one thing. It is certain that he steeled his will and drove ruthlessly forward to the goal he saw ahead of him. He was like that before he became a Christian, when he argued with Stephen and accused him before the council. The same fanatical zeal drove him to Damascus to wipe out the Nazarene sect. It tallies with the fact that as an apostle he struck down his opponents with a hard hand and foamed with rage against them: they were dogs, false brothers, hypocrites; their fate was perdition; they turned honour into dishonour. And although he was small of stature, he radiated authority. Paul was not an easy man to work with. There were disagreements between him and some of the best men in the church. On the other hand he warmed his congregations with loving tenderness; he was like a father, nay like a mother, to them. He was also solicitous about individuals;

he used tact and wisdom to make peace between a master and his runaway slave.

But again the contrast strikes us forcibly. If purity of heart means following the straight path to the goal, Paul sometimes showed impurities. He was a tactician. When he thought it prudent, he sailed a tricky course and was not always free from the taint of opportunism. Indeed, Paul was proud of adapting himself to changing conditions and made no bones about it: 'And unto the Jews I became as a Jew. . . ; to them that are without law, as without law . . . I am made all things to all men.' He rejoices with the joyful and weeps with the sorrowful and says frankly: 'Even as I please all men in all things.' It is not surprising that at times he had to defend himself against accusations of acting like a chameleon. Even present-day readers of his epistles are startled by contrasts in his ideas. Some of them had far-reaching consequences for both synagogue and church.

It is difficult to get to the bottom of Paul's character and ideas. After all, he belongs to a quite different world from our own. We children of the technical era know very little about the dark regions of mysticism. But if we want to plumb the depths of Paul's mind and the essence of his ideas, we must remember that he was a mystic—one of the greatest the world has ever known. The mystic is never troubled by the problem of the existence of the invisible world. That is the world he lives in; it is more real than anything he can touch and feel. And life consists in penetrating deeper and deeper into this hidden reality. That is why the heavenly vision on the way to Damascus was definitely not a psychological phenomenon that Paul tried to analyse, but something tangible; that is why he was proud of speaking more languages than the others and his preaching was not with 'enticing words of man's wisdom, but in demonstration of the Spirit and of power'. Nor must we forget that he had experiences that are foreign to present-day Christians. He felt himself 'caught up to the third heaven . . . and heard unspeakable words, which it is not lawful for a man to utter'.

Paul saw deep into God's hidden wisdom, for 'the Spirit searcheth all things, yea, the deep things of God'. Indeed a platform to stand and act on.

Such was the man whose words and deeds spread the gospel of Christ resurrected far and wide and made a distinction between old and new.

Tarsus in Cilicia was a large bustling city. One of the most important roads in the Roman Empire ran through Asia Minor, climbed over the Taurus mountains through the Cilician pass and continued further east by way of Tarsus. The city lay near the sea, and road and port made Tarsus a centre for trade and traffic. Here East met West. Greek and Roman culture mingled with the multi-coloured life of the East and together they created an atmosphere of typical Hellenism. Although the Jewish colony in the city did its utmost to isolate itself, it could not help being marked by its heathen surroundings. But a young Jew who grew up in Tarsus had a broader outlook than one who lived in the homeland with its strict orthodox Jewish life. He knew from his childhood that there was a world outside Jerusalem.

The young Saul of Tarsus was proud of being a Jew. He never forgot it, not even when he became a Christian. His home must have been a prosperous one. Saul was born a Roman citizen, something rare for Jews, because the privilege was only inherited in distinguished families. The Jewish spirit was strong in the family. Saul called himself a Pharisee of Pharisees. The word is in the plural, which means generations of Pharisees behind him. We realise that Saul imbibed true Judaism with his mother's milk. No sooner could the child read than he began to spell his way through the Torah, and his school impressed its regulations and commandments on him. The Torah became the heart of his faith.

But every time the lad ran outside his home's protecting wall, he was in another world, far removed from the one his family lived in. It was in the street and among foreigners that he listened to the rich flexible colloquial Greek we know from his letters. The watchful lad stood in the crowd around the philosophers at every other street corner and picked up words and aphorisms from their speeches; he listened curiously if someone spoke about the incomprehensible ceremonies of the secret and therefore doubly fascinating mystery religions. Hellenistic everyday life was displayed before his young impressionable mind; he shuddered at the sight of the countless statues of gods and altars of undisguised obscenity, but he was also an excited spectator of the competitions in the stadium.

We do not know whether his father decided to send his young son to Jerusalem out of fear of this influence. It was more probably because as a good Pharisee he wanted Saul educated in a rabbinical school, and the best place for that was at the feet of one of the great teachers in Judaism's metropolis. Many years later Paul could cry to the citizens of the holy city:

'(I was) brought up in this city at the feet of Gamaliel, and taught according to the perfect manner of the law of the fathers, and was zealous towards God.'

Those youthful years among the greatest Pharisees of the day left their mark for life. From his home Paul knew the Bible in the Septuagint's Greek translation; in Jerusalem he read it in the holy tongue and was trained in rabbinical methods of interpretation. Modern readers are surprised when they sit with Paul's letters and time after time come upon remarkable exegeses of events in the holy history. In the Epistle to the Galatians Paul says that the promises were made to Abraham and his seed, but emphasises that the word is in the singular, 'seed', not 'seeds'. He also gives an allegorical interpretation of Abraham's relationship to the two women, Sarah and Hagar, and attributes decisive importance to these things for the understanding of the revelation. We clutch our heads and do not understand what he is getting at. But we must remember that these and other similar explanations in Paul's work are rabbinical interpretations. They are typical of his time and were illuminating to his readers.

We others can be content to regard them as curiosities and let them stand for what they are. But at times they undeniably make the apostle's ideas complicated.

All this is of minor importance. It is far more important that throughout his life Paul testified that scholarship was not the stuff of memory or acrobatic dialectic, but became flesh and blood in him. Again and again we read that he believed in and acted according to the Torah and that he 'profited in the Jews' religion above many my equals in mine own nation, being more exceedingly zealous of the traditions of my fathers'. It was this burning zeal that drove him to his persecution of the church with all its consequences.

Frequently the most enthusiastic and ardent advocate of a cause is trying, often quite unconsciously, to hide inner uncertainty and silence his doubts by his zeal. Psychologically speaking, religious phenomena of this kind are so general that we involuntarily resort to such an explanation, if in fact we want an explanation, of the drama on the road outside Damascus, where Saul was suddenly transformed into Paul. But why seek a natural explanation when it was Paul's own explanation of the event that had lasting significance? And why doubt that God acts in a sovereign way when he chooses one of his great servants?

Paul became the Apostle of the Gentiles. That is the name the church gave him as an honour and he deserves to bear it. Paul was by no means the first man who made heathens believe in Christ resurrected. We have already seen that Peter and many others opened the church door when the heathens knocked at it, long before Paul. But these simple men had absolutely no idea of the consequences of the events that they set in motion by accepting Gentiles. They did not realise that many of the heathens' teeming millions were ready to stream into the church, and that in the course of a few decades they would give it a new face and tear it loose from the Judaism they themselves had been brought up in and had linked up with the new faith as a matter of course.

I

It needed a Paul to look these enormous problems in the face and tackle them.

Paul had grown up far away from Jerusalem and had breathed the air of Hellenism. He was a full-blooded Jew by birth and upbringing and education. From the moment that he became as completely a Christian as he had been a Pharisee before, he knew in his own mind the tension in the triad, Jew, Greek and Christian. If we believe that God in His wisdom chooses the tools He has use for, and forms and sharpens them for the end on which He intends to employ them, we have in Paul the classical example of what in a stale and often misused cliché is called the chosen tool.

During the church's two thousand years no one set his mark on it and stamped Christian thinking about salvation's mysteries as Paul did. As the Apostle of the Gentiles it is to his honour that the church set out from Jerusalem on a victorious campaign round the world, but it is also his responsibility that the break between the two sisters, synagogue and church, was as sharp as it was. He himself did not seek the disastrous break, but in his letters, successors who were not as great as he have found so rich an arsenal that they have always been able to find weapons for war against Israel.

So it is understandable that Jewish scholars can claim that Paul created a new religion, world-embracing Christianity, out of Jesus's teaching. 'Without Jesus no Paul. But without Paul no Christianity.' That is how Joseph Klausner puts it. And he carries the idea further in the bitter words that 'Judaism brought forth Christianity in its first phase, but it rejected its daughter when it saw that she embraced her mother in a fatal kiss'.

However, the matter is not so simple. No one should be surprised that there is a difference between Jesus and Paul. Jesus lived in narrow isolated Judaea, Paul in the broad Hellenistic world. Their backgrounds cannot be compared, and this drove their thoughts to follow paths that ran far apart from each other. Nor did their problems follow the same pattern, first because Jesus exclusively consorted with

Jews in Judaea, while Paul met men who were heathens but wanted to become Christians. Here Paul stood at a crossroads that Jesus never even reached.

At that time Christianity was still a Jewish sect and the burning question arose whether the Gentiles' way to God went by way of Judaism. Practically speaking: were heathens to be circumcised before they were baptised? And since Judaism is the Torah and the Torah is Judaism, the problem went further. Had Christians to observe the Torah? Yes or no? The church had to state its attitude to the Torah.

Throughout his life Paul struggled with this thorny question. And as he was the man of contrasts we saw him to be, he took it up under now one, now the other point of view; he twisted and turned and never let it go. New situations arose in the congregations; questions flowed into him and called for speedy answers. That is why we find widely differing ideas in his epistles when he writes about the Torah. Sometimes they contradict each other so flatly that we are surprised that the same man can have thought and written opinions that stand in striking contrast to what we read a few pages further on. In one place he says that 'by the deeds of the law there shall no flesh be justified in his sight', and 'if there is righteousness with the law, then Christ's death is in vain', yet in another he claims that the law is holy and just and good, and it is one of Israel's privileges that God's word is entrusted to it. Such glaring discrepancies were bound to cause difficulties both for himself and the church. We shall try to follow Paul on his winding road to find out God's purpose for Israel and the church.

In an earlier chapter we left Barnabas when he had found Paul at Tarsus and set out with him on the first missionary journey. The two missionaries ranged far and wide in Asia Minor. Everywhere they found men in whose minds the ground was ploughed and harrowed and lay open to receive the seed they sowed. They often succeeded in convincing Hellenistic Jews, proselytes of various degrees and god-fearing heathens. They gathered in the synagogues where Paul preached; many were baptised and new congregations sprang up. But the turning point came at Antioch in Pisidia. The Acts refer to Paul's sermon, in which in the proper rabbinical manner he expounded the holy story as the Scriptures tell it, but concluded with Jesus's death and resurrection. The forgiveness of sins was to be found through him and not through obedience to the Torah. The sermon made an impression; they asked Paul to come again on the next Sabbath and say more. But during the week genuine steadfast Jews had time to think over and discuss what Paul had said. When the Sabbath came, and the synagogue was packed full, they spoke loudly and critically against Paul. The meeting was in an uproar; caustic words flew through the synagogue like arrows. The result was that Paul made a great decision. He sprang up and cried:

'It was necessary that the word of God should first have been spoken to you: but seeing ye put it from you, and judge yourselves unworthy of everlasting life, lo, we turn to the Gentiles.'

Here we hear for the first time the note that was later to ring through his letters like an echo: 'to the Jew first, and also to the Greek'.

The words did not mean a definitive break between Paul and the synagogue; such great importance must not be attached to them, if only because Paul immediately began his work in the synagogue and among Jews again in Iconium, the first town he came to after Antioch. This became his fixed line of action wherever he went, but the words were an indicator that pointed to a crisis.

Scarcely had the two apostles returned to their headquarters at Antioch in Syria when the crisis exploded. The congregation there was a mixture of both Jews and Greeks, the latter forming the great majority. But the two kinds of Christians had always lived peacefully together and met each other at communal meals. That naturally meant that the strict Jewish dietary rules were not observed. When the rumour reached Jerusalem, a message was sent that such laxity and disorder could not be tolerated, and that heathens must be circumcised in order to become Christians. While Paul and Barnabas were away, Simon Peter had stayed in Antioch and led the community. Both he and Barnabas were frightened by the order from Jerusalem and withdrew from 'table-fellowship' with the Greeks. But Paul was furious. He attacked the two with sharp words and reproached them for their cowardice. Passions ran high. The congregation was divided on the subject.

But the question of 'table-fellowship' between Jews and Gentile Christians lay on the periphery; it was not the crux of the matter. The main point was Jerusalem's request for the circumcision of Gentiles who became Christians. The mother church obviously stood firm in its claim that the Torah was binding on Gentile Christians. Paul and his congregation countered it. One point of view opposed another and still an authoritative decision was not found.

The time was ripe for the church to speak as a church. This happened at the first council which was ever convened, the so-called apostles' meeting in Jerusalem, probably in the year 49. Paul and Barnabas were invited to go to the church's headquarters and meet 'the pillars', as Paul called the leaders with an ironical smile.

Councils are usually battlefields for conflicting opinions and this one was no exception. We read in Acts that there was 'no small dissension'. But the two missionaries came from the great world with news of remarkable experiences; they related 'what miracles and wonders God had wrought among the Gentiles by them'. Such accounts made an impression and the day was theirs. James spoke and accepted the point of view of Paul and Barnabas. No one could suspect this strict man of God of flirting with forbidden liberal ideas. When he had finished his speech and sat down, the decision was taken.

The council carried it unanimously and sent out letters to the congregations that 'it seemed good to the Holy Ghost, and to us' that the Gentiles had access to the church without first becoming Jews. The only obligation they had to accept were the seven Noachian commandments. Here the council was thinking of the commandments that were imposed on Noah's sons and which Jews regard as binding on all mankind. They forbid the worship of idols, murder and fornication, but when the council specifically referred to the Noachian commandments, it was not with a view to these axiomatic precepts, but because two of the other commandments made it easier for Jews to accept outsiders among them. They order abstention from 'things strangled', and consequently their flesh, which is not ritually slaughtered, but has blood in it. In the next place one must abstain from meat that has been offered to idols. In this way the apostles' meeting also held the door ajar for strict Jewish Christians, but on the main point the result was a victory for Paul. We never hear afterwards that the church went back on its decision.

But unanimity at the council did not mean that criticism of Paul was silenced. It grumbled and laid in wait in corners and continued as long as he lived. At times it broke out into bright flames; indeed once it put him in mortal danger. If Paul treated the Torah lightly where the Gentiles were concerned, it was an obvious step to suspect him of doing away with it for the Jews themselves. How dared he, a Jew, nay a Pharisee, interfere with the holy Torah! The slightest weakening of the Torah always aroused a storm of indignation.

Developments eventually proved these agitators right. Only a few generations were to disappear before the church rejected the Torah and Judaism but appropriated everything in it that it found of value. And the men of the church found support for this in Paul.

The apostles' meeting in Jerusalem only decided the Gentile Christians' relation to the Torah. It did not say a word about Jewish Christians also being free from it. Perhaps Paul thought it wise at this point to keep his ideas on the subject quiet. On other occasions we see him as an adroit diplomat; he knew the truth of the saying in Ecclesiastes that there is a time to speak and a time to keep silence. But if it was time to keep silence in Jerusalem, there came other times when he spoke. He did so in his epistles. But before we begin to look through them, let us look at the picture Luke paints of him in the Acts of the Apostles. From Luke we learn that in his personal life Paul felt bound by obedience to the Torah. He was a Christian, but he never let go of the Torah God gave his people on Sinai.

In the beautiful vivid book that Acts is, Luke sketches the apostle's life up to the time when he awaits the imperial court's decision about his case as a prisoner in Rome. In my opinion we can count on Luke, the intelligent educated doctor, as a reliable historian. Naturally the book must be read with watchful criticism. We notice that in places Luke has his own private intentions; he arranges his material and paints Paul's portrait with his own colours. But Luke was an eyewitness of many of the events he tells us about. Three long sections form the so-called 'We passages', where he himself was on the spot. All things considered, Luke is certainly right when he describes Paul as a law-abiding Jew.

This shines through especially on his last journey to Jerusalem. Paul was warned against going to the holy city. Dangerous enemies lay in wait for him, but he felt obliged, 'bound by the spirit', as he put it, to defy the danger. He knew that thousands of Christian Jews frowned on him and were infuriated because he taught the Jews who were among the Gentiles to desert Moses. So what could he not expect from zealous fanatical Jews who wanted to insult and punish him? For that very reason Paul emphasised his loyalty to tradition by taking a so-called Nazarene vow and 'being at charges' for others who had 'a vow on them'.

In spite of these security measures, the visit to Jerusalem ended in uproar and Paul's arrest; he escaped assassination by the skin of his teeth. During the dramatic events that we can read about in the Acts of the Apostles, Paul made a number of speeches, first in Jerusalem, later in Caesarea, in which he constantly emphasised his Jewish birth and faithfulness to Torah and temple. If his behaviour before his arrest and these speeches had not made a genuine and trustworthy impression, the Jewish Christian leaders would not have accepted him warm-heartedly, still less would the Pharisees have found him innocent. When the affair ended, the accusations against Paul were narrowed down from religious to political ones. It merely remains to add that immediately after having survived the dramatic winter voyage across the Mediterranean, he summoned the Jewish leaders in Rome and complained that he had done nothing that could harm the people or their fathers' customs.

In other words, Paul was a Jew. However much we twist and turn the problem, we end with the conviction that the great apostle never tore himself loose from his fathers' traditions and great past. To the end of his days Paul lived a Jewish life. He observed the holy-days and commandments, and earned his living by a handicraft, tent-making, like other Pharisees. When he wrote or preached, it was according to the methods he had learnt in his youth at Gamaliel's school. His argumentation resembled other learned rabbis' in knowledge and references to great figures in Israel's history—everything was just as it sounds in any synagogue. Only with the difference that Paul knew the name of Him for whose coming all Jews waited.

So much for the Acts of the Apostles; now for Paul's epistles.

We possess thirteen of them. They are preserved in the New Testament and they all probably come from his hand. There is uncertainty about one or two epistles and later copyists have undoubtedly made their private changes and additions here and there. But these doubtful cases do not count for much in a general evaluation of Paul's message to his congregations. The apostle certainly wrote many more letters than those we know. There are great gaps in our knowledge of his life and theology. But we must be content with what we have been given. The letters were preserved in the archives of the congregations they were addressed to. Gradually they circulated in wider circles and so ended up as important constituent parts of Christian Holy Writ.

Letters are letters. That has its advantages, but also its shortcomings. Our age does not write letters; we pick up the telephone. But if we had our telephone conversations recorded on tape, the result would be reminiscent of the letters of the past. Nothing is so revealing as listening to one's own taped telephone conversations or reading letters one wrote decades ago, one's hasty outbursts or spontaneous utterances. Letters provide snapshots of the mind and temperament of the person who writes them. We must not expect to find a balanced statement of the letter-writer's teaching in a letter. If we do, the letter is no longer a letter, but a thesis. It requires careful choice of words and considered argumentation. In its more important passages Paul's Epistle to the Romans is more a thesis than a letter.

No one should imagine that Paul dreamt for a moment that the letters he dictated in haste and the mood of the moment, some of them quivering with rage, others glowing with tenderness, would form part of the church's liturgy thousands of years later, nor that scholars would put them under the microscope and dissect them, discuss, argue about them and form schools based on their opinions, or that countless theologians would win doctorates by writing about them. Four hundred and thirty different interpretations have been given of one single word in the Epistle to the Galatians! And Paul knew that among his readers were 'not many wise men after the flesh, not many mighty, not many noble'. This phrase is from one of the Epistles to the Corinthians; the readers in Galatia were certainly no better. No, the more subtle nuances of his argument were over the heads of the recipients.

Such is Paul's background as a letter-writer. It would be quite unreasonable to assert that every word was inspired by the Holy Ghost with sovereign authority for all time. Here writes a highly gifted, perpetually restless man, who, in his solicitude for his congregations, struggles with the ideas that preoccupy him. The letters cover many years; they were written or dictated under widely differing circumstances. Now Paul emphasises one side, now the other. The gospel is spirit. It cannot be arranged like a time-table with exact times of departure for every train or worked out by a central office of information. It is infinitely great, like the perpetually changing sky, which is full of storm clouds one day and blue and clear in the next day's sunshine. It is in contrasts that the spirit's riches can be recognised. So the reader will understand that I am not pressing the contrasts in Paul's ideas to the limit, but letting each of the opposite poles tell its side of the eternal truth which is life's ultimate reality.

Where Paul is greatest and lets us see into the secret, the centre of his belief, one single thing towers over all others. Golgotha and the open grave have revealed God's plan for the salvation of everyone, both Jews and Greeks. In his belief in Christ, the awaited Messiah, Paul was transformed into a new man. Impotence became faith that allowed him to merge with the divine. The key words are 'in Christ'. In union with him, he is a limb of the holy church, which is the body of Christ. In him all frontiers are done away with; here is neither Jew nor Greek, bond nor free, male nor female; all are one in Jesus Christ. The whole creation is redeemed and divine love fills every nook and cranny of the man who is in Christ and turns again to the Almighty in humble thanks. In this genuine Christian mysticism we have Paul and the heart of his Gospel. All other problems must be considered in relation to it. However great they may be, they are small in relation to the greatest. That is even true of the problem of the church and Israel.

These are more than ideas, these are things lived through, experience. Paul's view of Israel and the Torah was born of dearly bought experience.

There are long passages in Paul's epistles which sound

strange and unintelligible to the reader who approaches them
without previous knowledge of his age's ideas and conception
of the world. It cannot be otherwise, for Paul's method of
expression is dated. Every book from another age calls for
work on the reader's part if he is to understand it. In the
same way, books and advertisements from our twentieth
century will one day seem strange to readers of later generations. But on the other hand there are sentences and passages,
indeed whole pages in the Pauline epistles, which are so fresh
and sparkle with such experience of beauty and joy, but also
with dread and horror, that they might have been written
yesterday. And the modern reader gives them a nod of recognition because he himself has been through the same thing.
This is not dusty wisdom from the study but a living
man's experiences. That is why many quotations from St.
Paul have become precious parts of mankind's cultural
inheritance.

One of the best-known examples is the description in the
Epistle to the Romans of the human mind's unfortunate division between good and evil, in which Paul found the Torah
implicated, and which drove him to reflections about his
place in God's household. Here are two quotations:

'For we know that the law is spiritual: but I am carnal,
sold under sin.

'For that which I do I allow not: for what I would, that
I do not; but what I hate, that I do.'

'I find then a law, that, when I would do good, evil is
present with me. . . .

'But I see another law in my members, warring against
the law of my mind, and bringing me into captivity to the
law of sin which is in my members.'

And doubt pours forth in a cry of misery:

'O wretched man that I am! who shall deliver me from
the body of this death?'

Here we read the classical account of the hopeless
wrestling-match between body and spirit, in which all good
intentions collapse before powers that are stronger than he.

We are given an insight into long years of experience. Once there was a happy childhood without shadows and mental conflicts, but when he got to know the Torah sinful lust awoke. That is how Paul remembered it beginning. And it shocked him that even God's Torah pointed to sin and aroused his desire. So confused is the human heart that the forbidden entices and leads astray. 'For sin, taking occasion by the commandment, deceived me, and by it slew me.' He felt as if he were under a curse.

This is Paul before Damascus, divided, unhappy, on the verge of collapse. No one else knew what he suffered; he showed a mask to the outside world. Otherwise the council would not have given him papers and full powers to wipe out the Nazarene sect in Damascus. He threw himself into the task; his only way out was ceaseless activity. Although weary unto death, Paul kicked against the pricks. Until he whom he least of all expected intervened. Then Paul yielded to Jesus and believed in him as the Messiah. In his belief in him he found what all his hankering after obeying the Torah had never given, the peace he later called righteousness through faith and not through works.

Paul never let go of this dearly won treasure. He built it into his system of ideas and fought for it wherever he saw it underestimated or misunderstood or misused. And because it was precious to him, he used sharp words. He would not have been Paul if he had spoken more gently.

Throughout his life Paul's thoughts revolved around God's purpose with the Torah. Its codex of regulations came from God's hand on Sinai; for more than a thousand years it had preserved Israel as God's people. But he knew from bitter experience that the Torah merely pointed out the way; it gave no help to the man who had to walk along it. Finally it became clear to Paul that the Torah was a taskmaster sending men to Christ. The shadow of consciousness of sin that was a consequence of the Torah would drive men to find salvation and redemption in the belief in the crucified and

resurrected Messiah, Jesus of Nazareth. That was Paul's way
from Sinai to Golgotha.

With Golgotha we touch the nerve of Paul's Christian
faith. And here the church's way left the synagogue's. From
now on the two ways ran in different directions. But at the
crossroads the Jew raised his finger and claimed that Paul's
teaching about Jesus's act of redemption was a heresy. He
revealed his Hellenistic background in it. The heathen
mystery religions' talk of nature's death in the winter and
reawakening in the spring, of a dying and resurrected
redeemer, entered Christian doctrine as Jesus's death and
resurrection, and the redemption he won.

It cannot be denied that Paul used ideas and expressions
he remembered from his childhood and youth in Hellenistic
Tarsus. It would have been unnatural if he had not, for that
was the air he had breathed. It was that that made him a success, to use a modern expression, among Gentiles and Hellenistic Jews. He was a man who spoke their own language. But his
dependence on Hellenism was limited to the language. The
ideas themselves stemmed from Paul's Jewish background.
The picture of the Suffering Servant of the Lord in the Book
of Isaiah told of redemption through suffering and death.
And there was one clear-cut difference between Paul and the
mystery religions. For them redemption was the final goal,
for Paul it was the first step. It opened the door to what really
mattered, union with the resurrected one in the body, of
which Christ was the head, and to living a righteous life.

Two ways radiate out from Golgotha. And Paul acquired
a following on his way. The majority were heathens, who—
to quote Virgil—stretched out their hands in longing to the
other shore. Followers also came from his own people, but
singly and in small numbers in comparison with the whole.
Never Israel as a people. For the Jew did not need salvation in
the same sense that Paul understood the word. The deep dark
dogma of original sin, born of bitter acknowledgement, says
that man is born with a 'night' side of evil. Before we existed,

we were doomed to sin. That was Paul's own experience.

But this idea is unknown to the Jews. Man is born pure, says Judaism, but with capabilities for both good and evil. He must choose between the two and he can do so, for the will is free. The art of being a man is to combat evil and win dominion over one's impulses and desires. That is why the Christian Golgotha-drama about salvation and redemption is foreign to the Jew; he has no use for a saviour. In the Bible's Hebraic language there is not a single word for salvation in the sense that Paul uses it. No, by obtaining help from God a man is able to conquer evil with his own forces. If he stumbles, he must seek his way back to Good through prayer and conversion and win forgiveness. With God's help man is in a position to obey the Torah. Judaism did not accept that it was permissible to teach sinners to despair because they did not observe the law and so needed a saviour. Therefore, the cross was a scandal to Judaism and he who hung on it accursed.

Justification by works and justification by faith form the tension between Sinai and Golgotha. And like the man of contrasts he was, Paul stayed in this land of tension throughout his life. He knew full well that faith does not replace the duty to live in obedience to God. The practical admonitions in his epistles indicate the Christian's duties. He himself remained a Jew and required his Jewish Christians to remain so too. The only exception he not only allowed, but required, was that communion between them and the Gentile Christians should not be broken by pedantic observance of the Torah's dietary laws. For the two had to be one. He expresses this in words which open up broad perspectives:

'For he (Christ) is our peace, who hath made both one, and hath broken down the middle wall of partition between us; . . . for to make in himself of twain one new man, so making peace.'

But the two *were* not one. That was the painful problem

Paul had to wrestle with. Like a blow in the face with a whip, it came home to him for the first time in the synagogue in Pisidian Antioch, when he saw unyielding faces and cold eyes among his fellow-countrymen. They were closed to the gospel of the crucified and resurrected Messiah, and wherever he went afterwards, the experience was monotonously repeated. How could he understand it? The prophets and apocalyptic books had ceaselessly predicted the Messiah's coming and each of them painted its own picture of him and the golden age he was to introduce. But no one, absolutely no one, had dreamt that Israel would meet him with disbelief when he came. Yet that became the cold reality. Even if the first Christians in the church were Jews and more Jews joined it daily, the fact remained that the important teachers and the majority of the people closed their doors to him. No Jewish mass movement towards the church was visible. To his amazement Paul saw two Israels step forward, the old and the new. The new, the Christian church, with both Jews and Greeks believing in Jesus Christ. But what of the old Israel? It was as if a knife had cut God's people in two.

In the course of the two thousand years which have elapsed since then, the church has come to terms with this state of affairs. All the more easily since it stole from Israel everything it had of value and which it considered as a legitimate inheritance from a dead person. But if we put prejudices and conventional ideas aside and project our minds back to that remote period, we begin to understand the tragedy in all its terrifying dimensions. Neither Paul nor any other Jew dreamt of the possibility of Israel being split. For Israel was a unity, a holy people, chosen by God for a special mission. The Messianic hope did not build first and foremost on Jews paying homage to the Messiah individually, but on the people doing so. Here the question was not one of individual, but of collective salvation. Being a Jew was no private matter.

Therefore Paul felt as if the knife that cut Israel in two was plunging into his own heart. 'I have great heaviness and continual sorrow.' Indeed, he could wish himself accursed for the benefit of his brothers, his kinsmen in the flesh. He trembled at the thought that God's word had failed. Then all faith would be swept away like chaff in the chill storm of doubt and rejection. In three famous chapters of the Epistle to the Romans, the ninth, tenth and eleventh, he tackles the problem and step by step he beseeches his way to God's answer to the problem.

There are not many passages in the New Testament that are studied and pondered over as these few pages are. Parts of them require a knowledge of the rabbinical technique of interpretation to be understood, others contain self-contradictions as glaring as those life itself forces on the man who dares to think, but in the midst of the darkness stands Paul as the seer, who looks forward through the mist to the end of time. Or—is he the brave warrior who is desperately banging his head against a door which the Almighty has locked and will only open at the hour he himself chooses?

No, for a few moments the door opens just enough for Paul to catch a glimpse of the hidden secret through the crack. God's word has not failed. The prophets never expected that more than 'a remnant of Israel' would believe. It is not physical descent from Abraham that makes Israel Israel and automatically gives Jews a share in God's promises. The true Israel is 'The Remnant', the seven thousand who did not bow the knee to Baal.

But Paul ventures even further. He sweeps all human merits aside and bows to God as the sovereign lord. 'It is not of him that willeth, nor of him that runneth, but of God that sheweth mercy.' God is the potter who makes one vessel unto honour and another unto dishonour. He calls and he rejects, as it pleases Him. In this connection Paul says bold words about the insoluble problem of God's foreknowledge and man's free will. As a Pharisee Paul was brought up on the idea that everything is foreknown and that man has free will. We find this contradiction in terms, which reflects human thoughts bankruptcy before life's immensity, in other places in Paul's epistles. Here it serves to explain that God has rejected Israel—and yet not rejected it, that He stands behind its obduracy, but turns its obduracy into belief.

The image of Israel as a good olive tree, whose branches are broken off because of disbelief to make room for wild branches to be grafted on to it, throws light on the problem for Paul. Rejection partly came upon Israel, so that the Gentiles' fulness could go in. But the image warns the church for all time against self-righteousness and smugness vis-à-vis the chosen people. Of God's grace alone did the wild branches find a place in the good olive tree and a share in God's promises. But God's grace can never be taken as a matter of course. Though it made the Gentiles heirs, it embraces Abraham's seed far more easily. For God has bound himself to them and 'the gifts and calling of God are without repentance'. One day the whole of Israel shall be saved. And Jews and Gentiles are on the same footing; all are concluded in unbelief so that God can have mercy upon them all.

Paul looks ahead to the end of time. The early church saw it as close at hand. The road only led round the next corner where Jesus's return in glory should be revealed. Paul's visions of Israel must be seen in this light.

This expectation was not fulfilled. Thousands of years have passed—and still God hides His last secret about Israel and the church. Paul caught only a glimpse of it. He understood that it was concealed in God's plan, for he ended his speculations by admitting that God's judgments were unsearchable and His ways past finding out. Like the Prophet Isaiah, he too could have cried out:

'Verily thou art a god that hidest thyself.'

When Paul died under the executioner's sword in Rome in the year 64, the church was still a Jewish sect. Paul never proclaimed an open break between synagogue and church. Like Jesus, he lived as a Jew all his life. Had he aimed at separating the church from Judaism, he would certainly have spoken more clearly about the matter than he actually did.

K

And he knew that the end was near, when the divided should merge with one another again. In other words, the schism was a brief parenthesis. It was not Paul, but the 'Paulinists' who made the break. That is what we can call his successors who seized on every single thought and idea that they found in Paul's epistles, as well as vague remarks and suggestions uttered in one specific situation or another, and turned them into rigid dogmas. Paul would shudder if they could be shown him.

The accusation that the Jews were behind Jesus's execution comes from the Gospels, which are later than Paul's epistles. We only find it once in Paul, in the Epistle to the Thessalonians. But it happened when he was angry with a congregation that had treated him badly. On the other hand, a couple of sentences in the passage from the Epistle to the Romans we have just mentioned saved the Jews from total annihilation in the Middle Ages. In them, it says that the conversion of the Jews is the prelude to the return of Jesus. So it was necessary to spare at least some Jews from compulsory baptism and the stake so that they could be converted at the right time. Otherwise Jesus would not come again!

Two years after Paul's death the great revolt broke out in Jerusalem. After four years' desperate warfare, it ended in the fall of the city and the temple's destruction in the year 70. The war put an end to peaceful co-existence between synagogue and church. We shall see later that a great Jewish teacher, Jochanan ben Zakkai, left the doomed city and in Jabne laid the foundations of a new Jewish centre which led the essence of Jewish faith and national life safely out of the catastrophe. The Christian church went the opposite way. Tradition says that it awaited the unfolding of events in Pella, east of Jordan. In its eyes the war was irrelevant; it only concerned the Jewish leaders.

Thus the war gave the signal for a definitive break. While the new council in Jabne considered Jerusalem's fall as God's punishment for the people's sin, the church knew that God had now removed the sceptre from Israel. Without the temple, the Jews had only the Torah left. And Paul's pupils considered the Torah as not only inadequate, but also superfluous, and its observance soon became a dangerous heresy. The ways parted and the books in the New Testament after Paul's epistles reflect the development.

The Epistle of James stands remarkably alone among the books in the New Testament. It does not go deeply into speculations about Christ, but emphasises in quiet language the importance of showing one's faith through works. There is a suggestion of a polemic against Paul in the epistle. Whereas Paul sets Abraham up as the Father of the Faith, James proves just the opposite, that the patriarch was justified by works, in that he was willing to sacrifice Isaac. Naturally Luther felt repelled by James's epistle; he called it a straw epistle. And there are scholars who assume that it was originally a Jewish product, which is used here in the service of Christianity. In that case it contradicts the undeniably prevalent saying that Judaism is sterile and dead.

The Epistle to the Hebrews seems to have been written immediately before the catastrophe in the year 70. It talks so intimately about the priesthood and temple services that both must still have been functioning, and it presupposes a knowledge of the ceremonies. Its aim is to convince the Jews that since Christ they no longer belong to the old covenant, but to the new one. The Torah is abolished; it was only a shadow, a copy of heavenly things, and Christ is the new high priest. The message of the Epistle to the Hebrews can be briefly expressed by saying that it recommends Christianity as the best religion. For it is better than the next best, Judaism.

We have already seen that the Synoptic Gospels gradually move further and further away from Judaism. The fourth Gospel raises the banner it fights under in one of its very first verses. 'He came unto his own and his own received him not.' Here no persuasion is attempted; the break is a fact. The battle-front is established; Christianity is the one true religion. It is the Gospel according to St. John that puts into Jesus's mouth the words 'No man cometh unto the Father, but by me'.

The last book in the New Testament, Revelations, was written when 'the sealed', i.e. the Christians, could be called the twelve tribes of Israel, without its sounding strange. Here the schism is accomplished. The church has finally adopted Judaism's methods of expression.

12 / FRONTS

SOMETIMES MEN ARE STRUCK BY A MISFOR-
tune that drives them to rapid flight. A prairie
fire sweeps roaring over fields and houses and
lays their homes waste, or barbarian enemies kill them with
fire and sword. If they want to save themselves, they have to
run for their lives and leave all their possessions behind them.
When they discover that the only way to safety leads through
a bog with treacherous bottomless depths, they have to cross
it from tuft to tuft. They hope that fortune will favour them
and strain every nerve to win through. If some miscalculate
a jump or a tuft gives way, they sink and the mud closes
over them. For others the venture is successful. The image
is that of Jewish destiny when Jerusalem fell. But for the next
two thousand years the Jews literally had to jump from tuft
to tuft to save their lives.

Jabne was the first tuft the road led across. Jabne is the
name of a little town that still exists today and lies south of
present-day Tel Aviv, in the middle of Palestine's coastal
plain, where the Philistines lived in ancient times. During
the momentous days of the year 70 a group of Pharisees,
young and old among them, gathered on a flat rooftop in the
town. They stood there motionless night and day, staring at
the reflection of the fires above the mountains in the east
where Jerusalem lay. The temple and the holy city were in
flames during the hours when Judaea's capital fell to the
iron-clad legionaries' massive onslaught. When the watchers

in distant Jabne learnt of the catastrophe, they rent their clothes, they sprinkled ashes on hair and beard and mourned as for a dead relative. But the eldest of them, whom the others looked up to as their leader, consoled them and said that now good works should take the place of offerings. Had not the prophet said that charity was better than offerings? Jochanan ben Zakkai was the man who pointed to the Jewish future with these words.

The story goes that the great teacher Jochanan ben Zakkai foresaw the end when he was in besieged Jerusalem and decided to leave the doomed city. Lying on a bier he escaped through one of the closely guarded gates. Jochanan shammed dead. His pupils, who carried the bier, had concealed a piece of bad meat in the grave-clothes. The stench drove the guards away in disgust. Jochanan achieved an audience with Vespasian, the Roman commanding officer, and was given Jabne as headquarters for his school. There he assembled a new Sanhedrin to govern the people and founded his academy.

The Jewish state collapsed, but Jochanan ben Zakkai saved the soul of Judaism. The work that Ezra and Nehemiah had begun five hundred years before was taken up by Jochanan and his many successors. They fostered and developed Jewish thinking and faith, so that Israel might live for ever in spite of all the catastrophes. Temple services and priesthood disappeared and the Sadducees with them, but the heart of Judaism survived.

The two centuries before Jerusalem's fall had seen a dangerous kind of inflation take shape in Israel. The people had expanded all too quickly and strongly; foreign elements, foreign both physically and culturally, had been more or less absorbed and that had required compromises. Out of the confusion new sects had grown up in profusion. Israel was parcelled out into schools which were at war with each other. Confusion had brought the people to the verge of annihilation. Only two sects survived the catastrophe. Pharisaism and Christianity. And they at once began to dig trenches against each other—or let us put it like this: they each found their way out over the tufts in the swamp.

In countries with centuries of history in their own land schools teach the growing generations the names and dates of former kings. Their names mark the nation's shifting destiny in vanished ages. What the Jews have to remember are not monarchs, but a stately series of great teachers, each of whom placed stones in the wall which guards Israel's estate. Jochanan Ben Zakkai's name stands as a milestone, but countless men followed in his footsteps. To name only a few of the best-known: Gamaliel the Second, Joshua Ben Hananiah, Rabbi Akiba, Jehuda ha-Nasi, in later generations Rabbi Shlomo Isaaci, known as Rashi, Moses Maimonides, Joseph Caro, Moses Mendelssohn and right down to our own time Martin Buber, Leo Baeck and Franz Rosenzweig. They were all learned men. And learning forms the aristocracy in Israel. The hero in Jewish legends is never the Christian St. George with his sword, but the learned man who kills the dragon of ignorance with shrewd thinking and superior knowledge. Not to be able to read is a disgrace; the ignorant man, whether he is rich or poor, is despised. A Jew marries his daughter more readily to a poor scholar than to the rich man who lacks education. And the men on the Jewish 'list of kings' had one thing in common: they all turned inwards to the thousand-year-old heritage left by Ezra and built Jewish faith on the Torah and the Talmud. The first centuries after Jerusalem's fall saw the Talmud take shape.

The academy in Jabne had its day. The next saving tuft lay in Tiberias on Lake Genesareth. But when the country knew terror again after Bar Kochba's (the Son of a Star's) war, the Jewish centre moved out of the Roman Empire and found a home with Rome's arch-enemy, in Mesopotamia under the Parthian Empire, which Rome never succeeded in crushing. And here by the banks of the Euphrates and the Tigris, in Sura and Pumbeditha and Nehardea, rose scholastic centres which played the same role in Jewish life as Oxford and the

Sorbonne and Harvard in Christian countries. Moreover, the Jewish universities became prototypes, patterns for the first Christian universities in the twelfth century. In them Jewish thought and culture became crystallised into the Talmud.

We have already seen how the Torah is one thing and the oral tradition another. But both have the same divine origin and root in the revelation on Sinai. The Torah contains 613 commandments, 365 of them say 'Thou shalt', the number of days in the year, and 248 say 'Thou shalt not', the number of bones in the body. The figures sound high, but they are actually modest. If the paragraphs in any European legal code were counted, we should be well on the way to a million. The 613 commandments lay down only the broad outlines of conduct in life; they need supplementing by specific regulations by the hundred thousand to cover every conceivable circumstance. On top of that, life never stands still; every new generation has its problems that require solution. That is why the oral law or the chain of tradition of the elders gradually grew up.

So a distinction is made between the written and the oral law. The latter is called oral because it went from mouth to mouth and was repeated endlessly until it stuck fast in the mind. For long ages it was forbidden to write it down. The teachers were afraid that even one written text would cast a shadow on the Torah's unique authority. They also knew that the spoken word has values that the written lacks. The latter brings thought to an end and closes the door to new ideas. We think of clergymen who 'preach' by reading a manuscript they have sweated through on Saturday night, and dare not venture into impromptu speech, with all its possibilities for fresh ideas and formulations that are born of mutual inspiration between preacher and congregation! Naturally the Jews of old were aware of this problem and helped to solve it by making a large part of their law oral. In addition there was the practical point that it was extremely expensive to produce books in ancient times. But in the end necessity drove the teachers to commit the tradition to paper.

The man was not born whose brain could house the mountain of material that had accumulated—indeed every time a Roman sword cleft a scholar's skull in two, three million words from Mishna and Gemara flowed into the gutter along with his brains!

It took centuries to write the Talmud down; the work went on in both Palestine and Babylon, so that we speak of the Palestinian and the Babylonian Talmud. The former was finished at the beginning of the fifth century, the Babylonian Talmud followed a century later. It appeared in several sections, first Mishna which means repetition, then Gemara, completion. In addition there is a large body of preaching and exegetical material, Midrash. Each group is divided into two main sections, Halacha, which means usage, and is a form of instruction in the law, and Aggada, full of legends and folklore and poetry. The Talmud was completed, but later ages went on working on it and made new commentaries and surveys. Judaism has always been in perpetual intellectual evolution and is anything but a dead letter. A short code of Jewish laws called Shulcan Aruch, which means prepared table, was written by Joseph Caro in the sixteenth century in Palestine's dream town Safed. It contains the most important rules and is a sort of pocket-book of Jewish life, an Everyman's Talmud.

The Talmud is not one book. It is sixty-three books or treatises, as they are called, usually collected in seventeen enormous volumes with a total of 15,000 large pages. One does not have to leaf through the work long to discover that the Talmud is not merely a series of heavy books, but a whole literature, the accumulation of a half or, more accurately, a whole, millennium's intellectual work covering many generations. If an outsider decides to penetrate the Talmud's strange world, he must be prepared for the work taking his whole lifetime. The Talmud's themes cover everything in life: law, ethics, medicine, logic, pedagogy, folklore, astronomy and zoology—not a single branch of life or knowledge is omitted. The Talmud can be called an encyclopaedia, a lexicon, but with the difference that in the Talmud all subjects are mixed and entangled in inextricable confusion. Halacha is commentaries and commentaries on commentaries and commentaries on commentaries on commentaries, and endless discussions about the problems that are commented on. The authors lived thousands of years ago; their outlook on life, the conditions they lived under, their trains of thought, methods and associations are so different from everything that we are accustomed to that the reader must enter completely into the spirit of them before he even begins to find his way. It is not surprising that the Jews build *yeshivot*, schools, in which young people are instructed in the Talmud.

Here is a sample of how Halacha gets its results. I have chosen an example that is also debated in our time. The Torah forbids the eating of 'carrion'. But what is carrion? The answer leads to finding the right method by which to slaughter animals. The decisive factor is not convenience, but an ethical principle. The animal must not be caused any pain. The Talmud asserts that an animal that dies while suffering or frightened, even during regular slaughtering, becomes carrion and therefore forbidden food. But what kind of death is painless? The rabbis, trained in medicine, found that animals die without pain if death is inflicted by a sharp clean knife in a single very fast cut that severs the two pulses in the throat. Moreover such a cut empties the animal of blood and fulfils the Torah's ban on eating meat with blood in it. For 'the animal's soul is in the blood'.

The Talmud is immensely old. And its age-old traditions, with obligations laid on the shoulders of the people who created such a monumental work, shaped the Jewish people. They lived according to its rules and endowed it with the eternal values that are won only through inheritance. We think of the American lady who asked the gardener of an Oxford college how he managed to keep the lawns so perfect, and the man's answer: 'The most important thing, madam, is to sow the grass 600 years ago!' For the Talmud is the accumulated wisdom of a people. No viewpoint in Hebraic thought is lacking; nothing human is alien to the Talmud. It appeared at a propitious hour, just as the Jewish people were preparing to start on the long wandering to countries whose names none of them knew and to face dangers no one could foresee. But wherever the Jews went, they took a father-land with them in the Talmud, not only a religion and a law, but also a culture. In it they possessed a world where they could settle and live their own lives, for it was protected by an insurmountable wall.

And one side of the wall formed a front against the Christian church. Silence. Silence about Jesus and about Christianity. That is the Talmud's dignified answer to the church's challenge. One must, as it were, follow a bloodhound on a leash through the Talmud's trackless undergrowth to find the rare references to Christianity and Jesus. Even then many of them are dubious. The Talmud's fathers must have known the truth of the saying that bad publicity is better than no publicity. Which is as much as to say that one strikes an enemy hardest by 'silencing' him to death. Even the vilest scandal or open abuse suggests that the author of it has felt himself attacked or contains a grain of positive criticism. Moreover, the Talmud is introspective. Its fathers' task was to 'cultivate the Lord's vineyard'; they turned their back on the outside world.

The silence was not total. It could not be, when we think of the church fathers' spiteful attacks on infidel Israel. Scat-tered through the Talmud we find passages saying that Jesus seduced Israel by sorcery, that he was the son of a Roman soldier and Mary Magdalene and was called Ben Stada or Ben Pandera. He lied when he called himself the Son of God. Mostly he is spoken of as 'the nameless one' or 'the bastard'. Details such as these produced the rank poisonous blooms which flourished in the Middle Ages in a book called *Toldot Yeshu*, the Generations of Jesus. It was a scandalous caricature of the Gospels, a merciless collection of calumny that circulated underground and only found readers in the lowest stratum of Judaism. But it must be seen as a thermometer that showed the high temperature of Jewish contempt for the church which acted so brutally against the Jews.

Even before the first century A.D. drew to a close, the Jewish authorities found themselves forced to take action against the church and erect a barrier between themselves and it. For a long time the Christians in most places were a Jewish sect. Christians took part in the services in the synagogue and profited, under Judaism's wings, by being members of a *religio licita*, a permitted religion, with the privileges that conferred. Now the synagogue wanted to get rid of them. At services in the synagogue, a series of prayers, *Shemone Esre*, the eighteen, is recited. Every person in the synagogue says them silently and with eyes closed; no profane word must interrupt them. Afterwards the leader of the divine service repeats them all aloud. Now a new prayer was introduced into this series, directed against *minim*. The word means heretics and designates the Christians. And since Christians could not take part in this prayer they found themselves forced to stay away from the synagogue. For the prayer ran: 'May no hope be given to the minim but may their wickedness perish instantly. May all thine enemies be destroyed and may thou speedily tear up the proud ones by the roots and humble them at this time.'

Letters went out to all the synagogues in the diaspora with warnings against the Christians and orders to introduce the new prayer into divine service. The synagogue had put the church at a distance.

Minim,[1] heretics. No hope for them, let them perish, be destroyed, torn up by the roots and humbled. Yes, the rabbis used strong words when they warned their flocks against the Jewish Christians, the Nazarenes, as they were called in Palestine. The council realised the danger they represented. As

---

[1] The word *minim* was later altered to *malshinim*, i.e., from heretics to slanderers. This is the phraseology used in today's prayer book.

long as they went to the synagogue and frequented orthodox
Jews' houses, they formed a fifth column. And they had undeniably good cards in their hand in discussions with their
fellow-countrymen when they pointed to the ruined temple
and reminded them of Jesus' prediction. It had been fulfilled
with terrifying accuracy, for literally not a stone had been left
standing on another. Was that not evidence that Jesus the
Messiah had introduced a new era? Christian doctrines crept
into the synagogue. There were passages which the Nazarenes
quoted so often that even the reading of them evoked recol-
lections of their Christian interpretation. Characteristically
enough, the prophecy in Isaiah 53 about the Suffering Servant
of the Lord was omitted when the chapter was read aloud
during the service in the synagogue. The verses before and
after were read, but not that passage, because it was one of the
Christians' main proofs that the crucifixion had been predicted by the greatest of the prophets. There were also stories
of Jews who believed in secret. A man lay dangerously ill
and one of the oldest Jews whispered in his ear. 'Believe that
the Son of God was crucified and will come again to judge
the living and the dead.' At another deathbed, the words
were: 'The crucified Jesus will judge thee.' Wherever death
knocked at the door, the secret Christians threw off the mask.

Such examples tell of Christian infiltration. They explain
the rabbis' sharp reaction. Today we are surprised that they
could include curses on people with other faiths in their
prayers. The eighteen benedictions were supplemented by
an anathema. But the excommunication had the desired
effect. The Nazarenes stayed away from the synagogue and
the rabbis' flock went about their everyday life out of the way
of infection from the Nazarenes.

The Son of a Star's war in the years 132-35 cut the last
bond between the old-fashioned orthodox Jews and the Christian Jews. The age's greatest Jewish authority, Rabbi Akiba,
supported Bar Kochba, and a large part of the people followed him. The Nazarenes naturally rejected him. The only
Messiah was the resurrected Jesus; Rabbi Akiba, they con-

sidered, ought to be struck blind if he called the rough
warrior Messiah. The Nazarenes withdrew, as they had done
during the first great war against Rome. They had to pay for
it with their blood, for they were persecuted mercilessly by
Bar Kochba's soldiers as long as they were in power.

When Rome had crushed the revolt and taken a bloody
revenge, everything was different in Palestine. The victorious
Emperor Hadrian closed Jerusalem to the Jews. He even
changed the name of the Holy City to Aelia Capitolina and
filled it with temples dedicated to Roman gods. And although
he treated the Nazarenes mercifully—after all they had not
taken up arms against Rome—they were weakened by war
and persecution and fell into the background.

For them the Son of a Star marked an epoch. The Gentile
Christian church made its entry into Jerusalem; a bishop
from the church's victorious wing took over the government.
The Nazarenes looked on the newcomers with misgiving and
isolated themselves. Their horizon narrowed; bitter antago-
nisms grew up in an atmosphere of provincial acrimony. Conflicts split them up into small sects which scowled fiercely at
one another. They did have certain things in common. They
observed the Torah, but rejected Paul's epistles. The apostle
was an apostate. They looked on Jesus as the son of Joseph
and Mary; the turning point in his life did not come until
his baptism. The only Gospel they recognised was Matthew's,
which does in fact bear the impress of Judaism most. We can
sum up their faith by saying that for them Christianity was
purified Judaism.

The Nazarenes were crushed to death between the
shields of the waring factions. The synagogue called them
minim and excommunicated them. And the vital rapidly ad-
vancing church sped past them and also came to consider
them as heretics. Cut off from both the victorious camps, all
alone in no-man's-land, they wasted away. Significantly
enough, the members of their most important sect were called
Ebionites, the poor. The name hits the mark, both literally
and metaphorically. It is tragic to think that the mother's

womb that once bore the Christian church of the future had
to wither. Today the Nazarenes are forgotten; even their
memory is lost in the mists of time. The tuft in the swamp on
which they sought a foothold gave way; they vanished into
the depths. They could have been bridge builders between
synagogue and church, but they were not equal to the
task.

We have followed the history of the Jewish front's stiffen-
ing and unyielding attitude to the church. But the church
also found a path that ran far away from the synagogue's, and
hostility, fostered by self-assertion and folly, flashed out
against the church's elder sister. The synagogue turned inwards; it closed its doors to the outside world. But the church
sallied forth among the Gentiles to harvest them into its barn,
and in order to hold their own and be intelligible out there,
its men had to enter into the spirit of and learn to use philosophical and religious concepts that were foreign to, and quite
different from, the Bible's. Already in St. Paul we find traces
of such efforts. But as early as the second century A.D. and
increasingly as time went by, not only was a new phraseology
used by the church, but alien thinking also filtered into ecclesiastical preaching and literature, and even into the church's
creed. Of course, the Bible always remained the church's
foundation, but Greek influence penetrated the development
of its ideas and dogmas to such an overwhelming degree that
we can talk of a marriage between Christianity and Greek
philosophy. Anyone who wants an example has only to compare the frank simple language of the Apostle's Creed with
the philosophical categories that make its successors, the
Nicene, Athanasian and Nicene-Constantinopolitan creeds,
grate on the ears of anyone familiar with the language of the
Bible.

All these were inevitable phases in the development the
church had to go through. Unfortunately, what served its
purpose at one time, in the long run locked Christian thought
up in a prison. Christianity was intellectualised; it rose into

a rarefied stratum of air far from the Hebraic spirit's personal and direct contact between eternity and human apprehension. On this score the church has paid dearly for the break with Judaism.

Here we touch on the early church's quarrels over dogma, a long and complicated chapter in its history. There were many individuals, indeed whole religious communities, who yielded. They foundered in Gnosticism and Neoplatonism and other semi- or three-quarter pagan 'isms' and disappeared for ever. It is one of the puzzles in Christian history that at times of crisis men were always called forth who found a way to save the essence of the church and Christianity from destruction. They stood at turning points where we again and again sense help from on high. But every time it happened, the front against Judaism was intensified. Out of the vast wealth of material we can choose a few examples which tell of this tragic side of what is in so many ways an elevating saga.

Justin Martyr lived in the middle of the second century. He was a Palestinian, born in the Hellenistic town of Flavia Neapolis, a new name for the ancient Shechem (today's Nablus). In his youth Justin sought wisdom in Greek philosophical schools, but when he was living alone by the sea in his middle age, he met an old man who directed him to the prophets and Christ. Convinced of the truth of Christianity and with all his Greek philosophy intact, he stands as a typical pioneer in the attempt to merge the two. He found that the pagan philosophers had borrowed the best of what they possessed from the Bible. Everything they taught about morality, the immortality of the soul and rewards and punishments after death was taken from it. The Bible's grain of truth had flown far and wide; 'all the magnificence that is found among the heathens, belongs to us,' he said. Justin bears the name of martyr because he gladly suffered death for his faith.

Justin Martyr met the Jew Trypho at Ephesus and entered into a discussion with him about which religion was the true one. We know the famous conversation, because Justin wrote it down in his *Dialogue with Trypho the Jew*, and the book has survived the many centuries that separate us from it. Naturally Christianity emerges victorious from the encounter. Nevertheless Justin was forced to apply a mute to the strings; he did not have it all his own way in the controversy. For he knew no Hebrew and only knew his Bible from the Septuagint Greek translation, whereas Trypho was a learned Jew who was never at a loss for an answer. But Justin simply took the Bible from him and called it 'your Bible, or more accurately ours, for even if you read it, you do not capture its spirit'.

With these words Justin initiated a campaign against Judaism that all subsequent teachers of the early church followed up. For them the Old Testament became a gold mine from which they took proofs of Christianity's truth and its superiority to Judaism. They had to interpret passages in the oddest ways, but they were never ashamed of using it to prove Christianity older than Judaism. It dated from the creation itself, whereas Judaism only began at Sinai. And even though Justin, unlike most of his successors, did not use directly hostile words against Trypho, he stands as a pioneer of the Christian polemics which widened the gulf between synagogue and church.

The fiercest and most radical enemy of the Jews, and the man who produced the most far-reaching consequences, was the heterodox Marcion, who lived at the same time as Justin. After his time the word Marcionism was used for total rejection of Judaism. Marcion was a fiery soul, an enthusiastic supporter of asceticism. From him stems the unhealthy remoteness from the world that had far too free a rein within the church. Marcion disrupted the community in Rome and was on the verge of leading the whole church dangerously astray.

His main work is not called *Antitheses*, i.e. opposites, for nothing. In it he splits the whole story of the revelation into two halves, which stand in relation to each other like fire to water, the Old Testament against the New, Judaism against Christianity. They are so different that they do not even have the same God. Judaism's God, Jehovah, is the God of this

L

world, the God of the Law, angry and judging. He created
the world, which is as evil and hard as Himself. He promised
His people, the Jews, a Messiah, and the latter was to appear
as Antichrist. But the highest God, who is the good one, takes
the creator of the world by surprise and has mercy on mankind. In an incarnation He reveals himself through Jesus
Christ and summons men to Him. The indignant Jewish God
nails Christ to the cross, but Christ overcomes Him in the
kingdom of the dead and will finally destroy his Messiah.
After the victory, the souls of the saved, but not their bodies,
enter His kingdom.

With this fantastic theology Marcion abolishes the whole
of the Old Testament and is naturally forced to do violence
to the New Testament as well. In his version it consists of
the Gospel and the Apostle. The Gospel is a mutilated Gospel
according to St. Luke, in which the passages that mention
the Jews, for example Jesus's entry into Jerusalem, are cut
out. The Apostle consists of two of the Pauline epistles, with
emphasis on Paul's debate with Simon Peter at Antioch. Paul
is, of course, his principal character.

The moment of truth in Marcion is his vision of Christianity's originality, its newness and independence, but his
teaching is a caricature of Paulinism. Marcion had far-reaching importance. His daring to take a critical look at Holy
Writ was something new that was not resumed in a thorough
way until modern times. Some of his ideas inspired Schopen-
hauer's philosophy. But in the early church he stands as the
man who dug deeper in the chasm between synagogue and
church than anyone else.

The fathers of the church is the name for the series of
great men who showed the church the way over the swamp's
treacherous tufts and led them safely through a long series
of mortal dangers. They are remembered and honoured in
the history of the church, and we believe that they were sent
by God. But in all their greatness we must not forget their
prejudice and narrow-mindedness, indeed evil fanaticism,

whenever they were confronted with Israel. It runs like a red
thread through all their writings that they never tried to
understand Judaism, but in their bitter disappointment over
its obstinate rejection of the Gospel were tempted to use
weapons against it that were far removed from the sword of
the spirit that Paul had urged them to wield in the good
fight for the faith.

Adversus Judaeos (Against the Jews) is the title of a
group of works by Tertullian, Cyprian, Hippolytus, Chrysostom and Augustine. As a Christian I am ashamed to quote
them, but the truth must be told. Even though antisemitism
does not shine through them all the time, it is found regret-
tably often. Chrysostom was one of the early church's intellectual figures and its most famous preacher. He well deserved
his name, which means golden-mouthed. In Antioch he
preached eight sermons against the Jews which are so full
of poison that the reader cannot believe his eyes. Here is one
of many examples: 'The synagogue is a brothel, a hiding-
place for wild animals. No Jew has ever prayed to God; they
are all possessed by devils. Instead of greeting them, ye shall
avoid them as a contagious disease and plague'. His sermons
concluded with the words: 'I hate Jews'.

Another of the church's great men distinguished between
'Hebrews' and 'Jews' in the Bible. All the honest figures in
the scriptures were Hebrews and forerunners of the Christians; the bad characters were Jews. The pious fathers read
the Bible in such a way that every time heresy or sin was
mentioned, the Jews were responsible, while heroic and devout men foretold the Christians who were to come. A quotation from one of their books speaks for them all. In the
following lines 'they' means the Jews:

Moses they cursed, because he proclaimed Christ,
Aaron they rejected, because he gave them the image of
Christ,
David they hated, because he sang of Christ,
Saul they exalted, because he did not speak of Christ,
Samuel they cast out, because he did speak of Christ,

Jeremiah they stoned, because he sang psalms about Christ,

Isaiah they sawed asunder, because he proclaimed his honour,

Judas they loved, because he betrayed Christ.

With this spirit behind the church's attitude towards Israel, it is not surprising that the Jews' worst time was ushered in by the church's victory and its position as the official state religion. The church's policy towards the Jews can be summed up in Rehoboam's words when the kingdom was split after King Solomon's death:

'My father chastised you with whips, but I will chastise you with scorpions.'

13 / GUILT

THE ROMAN CATHOLIC CHURCH CONSIDERS
Innocent III as the foremost of the 260 popes
who have ruled the church. Armed with St.
Peter's keys and the power the symbol conferred, he raised
the papacy from impotence and humbled the Christian kings
in Germany, Spain, France and England. The only one who
dared to speak out against Rome was King Sverre in distant
Norway. Before Innocent's day the Pope was only called the
Vicar of St. Peter. Not for nothing did he now become the
Vicar of Christ. But in our history the great Pope is remembered for the council he convened in the year 1215, the so-
called Fourth Lateran Council. Among many other problems
the council decided on was the church's attitude towards the
Jews, and a tragically negative attitude it was. It introduced
the Jewish badge. From then on all Jews over the age of thirteen had to wear a badge on their clothes showing that they
belonged to the despised people. The badge was round and
yellow, that is to say it was shaped like a coin and symbolised
the thirty pieces of silver Judas received for betraying Our
Saviour. Another theory was that it resembled the sacred host.
The Jews had refused to take part in the Last Supper. Now
they were forced to wear its symbol over their hearts.

The ostensible reason for the Jewish badge was that the
church wanted to prevent mixed marriages and so destroy the
links between Jews and Christians. It served as a warning
to the Christian, so that he or she could know who the partner
was. But the real intention went much further. The Jewish

badge was the mark of Cain which was branded on the Jew's forehead. He belonged to a pariah cast and was excluded from the company of other men, degraded to a life of isolation and contempt. The yellow badge took away his former pride and made the Jew a second-class citizen. It could be seen from his personal appearance. He crept through the streets with stooping shoulders and servile look; young lads threw horse-dung at him; jeers followed his shadow. Even in his own eyes he became what the priests did their best to turn him into: a contemptible and loathsome creature.

The year 1215. We have jumped a millennium from the time when the separation of synagogue from church became visible to everyone, and prejudice and resentment began to grow. During that thousand years the world had been shaken by revolutionary events; everything had changed—except the church's view of the Jews. That obstinate people, those obdurate refusers, were still standing outside the church and its salvation. Even when the classical world fell into ruins and the church emerged victoriously from the catacombs to ascend the throne, the Jews kept their doors locked. Europe's young barbarian nations were rapidly converted to Christ. But the Jews did not allow themselves to be infected by the example. In proud conviction of their inherited faith's superiority they looked down on the heathen peoples whose masses bowed down to the one yet threefold God.

Outside. One of the great church fathers formulated the consequence of such unbelief. *Extra ecclesiam nulla salus,* No salvation outside the church. So the once chosen people was rejected by God; they were placed under a curse and their magnificence taken over by the church, the new Israel. Everything good in the Old Testament referred to the Christians; everything bad to the Jews. The responsibility for the most horrible of all crimes, the crucifixion of God's only begotten son, would always cling to the Jews, those *deicidii*, killers of God. Demonic power must lie behind the Jews' rejection of Christ. A sinister atmosphere surrounded the incomprehensible and puzzling people. Zealous priests and monks pointed

at the Jews and told terrifying stories about them. They succeeded in uniting the people's fear and hate with their
cupidity for the Jews' possessions—an evil brew that boiled
over or exploded into horrible actions.

The church's official leadership tried to hold back. About
A.D. 600 Pope Gregory the Great gave a warning against forcible methods applied to the Jews. Compulsory conversions
were seldom effective. He ordered Christians to remember
that the Jews were evidence of the truth of the Scriptures;
their degradation showed that guilt was punished. Naturally
the church had to keep them at a distance. A Christian was
forbidden to go to a Jewish doctor, and Jews were never to
be entrusted with public office. Six or seven centuries later
St. Thomas Aquinas expressed the same view concisely and
clearly: the Jews must not be exterminated, but they must
always be humbled.

There is a degree of moderation in such words. But it
proved impossible to practise such moderation always and
everywhere. The church had called evil forces into being and
was unable to curb them. We come to the blackest chapter
in the church's long history. It concerns all sections of the
church: the Roman Catholic, the Protestant and the Graeco-
Roman churches. There was nothing to choose between them.
By means of distorted theology that was a caricature of interpretations of the Old Testament and by squeezing St. Paul's
epistles for details he never dreamt should have such consequences, the church piloted the very people from whom
salvation had come out into solitude and isolation, and left
them a defenceless prey to evil instincts. But the climax was
not reached until our own time. If modern antisemitism managed to grow as big as it did, it was because it had germinated
in soil the church had prepared, and drew weapons for its
propaganda from arsenals the church had placed at its dis-
posal. Sooner or later twisted ideas and poisonous words used
for millennia exact payment. Six million murdered Jews finally paid it. For the image of the gas chambers and smoking
crematoria chimneys in Hitler's concentration camps is the

receipt for the church's debt to the Jewish people. It is inconceivable how the church can escape the settlement on the great Day of Judgment when the books are opened and the accounts made up.

But if we are to follow history's account of synagogue and church, we are forced, humiliating though it may be, to take a look at details of the tragedy in which the introduction of the Jewish badge was only one incident.

A pope introduced the Jewish badge. At the Synod in Clermont in A.D. 1095 Urban II made his famous speech about freeing the Holy Land from the Saracen's power. *Deus lo vult*, God wishes it. That unanimous answer from the enormous crowd rang out under the open sky. A great idea drove the people of Europe together. The Crusades literally revolutionised every branch of the occident's life and thought. But for no one were the effects so marked as for the Jews. Fire and sword at once swept down on them. Many crusaders had sworn to revenge Christ's blood on the Jews before they went into battle. They found it absurd to leave Christ's oldest enemies in safety behind the front while they themselves risked their lives in the struggle against the infidels. The cry 'Hep, hep!' rang out in the big Jewish districts in the towns along the Rhine, and every kind of atrocity struck their inhabitants. The Jews were forced to choose between baptism or death. Most chose death. The campaign left bloody traces behind it the whole way to Jerusalem. In the holy city itself hardly a single Jew survived.

After the Crusades Europe's Jews lived in a constant state of fear. No one knew when he might have his house burnt over his head or be killed by an infuriated mob or be driven out on to the highway with his wife and children to look for a new place to live, if one could be found, or die in a convenient ditch.

An endless series of catastrophes for the Jews come under the heading of ritual murder. Behind the words lurked the suspicion that the Jew needed Christian blood for his rituals.

At Passover he stole a Christian child, cut its throat and baked the blood in his unleavened Passover bread. The accusation is as old as the Jew in the diaspora and has followed him right down to the present day. Examples are numerous; they can be told of many countries. There have always been a few people who willingly believed the rumour. Indeed, we know of people who increased its credibility by murdering a child themselves. They hid the corpse in a Jewish house. On Good Friday morning they 'found' the child and carried it through the streets held high so that everyone could see the gaping wound. I need not go into details of what happened to the Jews in the town.

The rumour smelt of blood. And when once the thirst for blood is aroused, it is not easily quenched. There was a great deal that aroused dormant suspicion of a town's Jews. No one really knew much about them. They kept to themselves. There was something mysterious about them that aroused uneasiness. If a Christian happened to peer into a Jewish home on Passover eve, he discovered that the family drank red wine. If he listened, he could catch isolated sentences that made him shudder. They intimated that the red colour was connected with blood. It certainly was, but not with Christian blood. No, the ritual was supposed to remind the Jews of the blood countless generations had poured out when they gave their lives for their faith.

But there were other things that seemed mysterious. The Jews took great care that the Passover bread, the so-called matzo, was prepared absolutely clean and free of yeast. So they surrounded the baking with complicated ceremonies, the meaning of which outsiders did not grasp. And what was more natural than to compare these matzot with the wafers the church uses for the Eucharist. Now it turned out that the Fourth Lateran Council that introduced the Jewish badge also introduced the Catholic dogma that the bread and wine of the Eucharist are actually transformed into the body and blood of Christ (the doctrine of transubstantiation). Suddenly it seemed obvious to suspect the Jews of stealing a consecrated host at Easter-time. In that way they had an opportunity to lay hands on the Saviour once again. For the church did say that the host was Christ. What a diabolical pleasure to stab and mutilate him!

Consequently an atmosphere of uneasiness and suspicion hung over the towns in which Jews lived. A spark could send the powder keg exploding into the air. And the sparks flew thickly. As soon as something inexplicable and unfortunate happened, it was the Jews' fault. Conflagrations raged ominously in the medieval towns with their tightly packed inflammable houses. Who had started the fire? The Jews, of course. If the enemy invaded the country, especially if it was the infidel Turks, the Jews had allied themselves with them and conspired. At Easter the atmosphere was thick and tense. The memory of the first Good Friday awakened.

But no atrocities can be compared with the one that struck the Jews during the epidemic about the middle of the fourteenth century, the Black Death. For they were the ones who had poisoned wells and springs and produced the plague. Jews were murdered or burnt in droves. In Germany, which has always been the country of mass psychosis, fear of the Jewish poison gripped people in a way reminiscent of the hydrophobia which follows the bite of a mad dog. At this time flagellants wandered from town to town. They were people rendered senseless by fear; they whipped themselves, stood in the street and cut themselves with knives, castrated themselves, while the horror-stricken spectators watched them. The Black Death was a time of terror. The plague killed millions, but it also demoralised the survivors, and the end was worse than the beginning.

Who were the rabble-rousers and rumour-spreaders in these incredible events? Yes, they were zealous monks and priests. They spread the poison from the pulpit, in the street and at home. Of course, they believed what they said. For centuries the church had become entangled in this web of suspicion and revenge. Its great men followed faithfully in the church fathers' footsteps. The Jews had murdered Christ;

they were cursed by God and had to be humbled until, when the end came, they could announce the return of Christ by their conversion. Since generation after generation of ordinary priests and monks had been brought up in such ideas, they considered it a service to God to popularise them among the common people and embellish them with all kinds of rumours and fabrications. Once they had gone so far, no earthly power was able to put out the fire that passions had lit. Naturally no pope wanted to see Jews flayed, tortured or burnt to death. Often enough a pope had the latest rumour of ritual murder investigated and came to the conclusion that it was unfounded, unprovable. But the lie had got a start and the people believed in it.

Ritual murder, violation of the host, the urge to find a scapegoat, the Inquisition. Each one of the words conceals tears and despair. The long list was finally crowned with the introduction of the ghetto. It was a pope who decreed it.

On July 12, 1555, a date in Christianity's history which is like a malignant boil, Paul IV issued the Bull *Cum nimis absurdis*. In cruel words it emphasised the absurdity of leniency to the Jews, revived the medieval ecclesiastical legislation against them and made certain innovations. The most important of the barbaric regulations was that henceforth Jews had to live cut off from Christians in a special street or quarter, isolated from the rest of the town by a wall. The bitterest humiliation was that the Jews inside the ghetto were forced to go to a house for catechumens. This was an ecclesiastical conversion centre where monks instructed Jews in the Christian faith and which they were forced to attend. Before the Jews entered the catechumens' house, their ears were examined to make sure that they were not stuffed with cotton-wool. And the servants in the hall were responsible for seeing that no one fell asleep. They did this by prodding the congregation with sharp sticks.

Pope Paul IV was the standard bearer of the Counter-Reformation. Martin Luther had shaken the Catholic church.

The Reformation conquered important countries in Europe. One might have thought that it brought the hope of good news from the church to the Jews, but it was only a transient breath of relief.

In the first years of the battle when the Reformation's fate still hung in the balance, we note Luther's sympathy for the people who have suffered most from Catholic fanaticism as long as men can remember. He broke with the medieval view of the Jews as Christ's murderers and called them 'Jesus's brothers in the flesh'. But Luther's friendliness to the Jews did not last long. He had calculated that the purified Christianity he professed and which drew inspiration from the Bible—which first belonged to the Jews—would draw them into his fold *en masse*. Once Luther realised that his gospel had absolutely no attraction for the Jews, he changed towards them. And his change was complete. It was as if the cloak fell from the reformer and revealed beneath it the embarrassing nakedness of the former monk, who displayed his inherited and deep-rooted hatred of the Jews to such an extent that it still staggers us. It seems like a pathological phenomenon. One can call it Judaeophobia, a morbid loathing of the Jews. And to any man who belongs to a church that bears his name, it is extremely humiliating to think that *the father of the church* lapsed on so important a point. For it was a lapse, indeed apostasy, not only from the ideas of Luther's youth, but also from the Lord of the Gospel he otherwise preached.

In the course of time Luther's writings became an inexhaustible arsenal for antisemitic propaganda. But his harsh words also had immediate consequences for the Jews. In the many religious wars that followed in the wake of the Reformation, they found themselves between the devil and the deep blue sea. The Protestants gave no quarter, but suspected them of secretly helping the Catholics. The Catholics, for their part, established that the whole accursed Reformation could be traced back to Jewish influence. The Protestant churches have never really freed themselves from the poison

Luther injected into their veins. Now and then a severe attack of fever breaks out. It happened, for example, to Adolf Stöcker, court chaplain in Berlin under the German empire at the close of the last century. And a slight feeling of distaste always makes the average Christian blush if he finds himself in the presence of a Jew. This minor manifestation of anti-semitism has never been eradicated.

The Russian church forms a chapter on its own. In it the word *pogrom* was created. It means 'destruction', but stands in all modern languages for mass persecution of the Jews, organised, or at least looked on sympathetically, by the authorities. One of the latter was the head of the Holy Synod, Constantin Pobedonostsev, who declared with cynical frankness that the solution of Russia's Jewish problem was possible only by forcing a third of the empire's six million Jews to flee, forcing the second third to the baptismal font and wiping out the remainder by starvation. But death by starvation takes time. Why not speed up the process by simply killing people? Right up to the First World War the Russian Jews' history is a long-drawn out account of discrimination, oppression, murder and degradation. No one should be surprised that the Jews reserved one of their bitterest curses for the Tsar: *Yemach shemo!* May his name be obliterated! or that a high proportion of the Bolshevik Revolution's leaders were Jewish. Finally, it should be noted that the Red Tsars inherited the White Tsars' policy with regard to the Jews and have continued it, at the time of writing, at any rate. But that is another story.

We have followed some of the stages in a thousand year long history of the church's debt to the Jews. But this matter does not belong only to history, nor is it an academic dissertation about an interesting but regrettable phenomenon. Time and again the church's attitude towards the Jews emerges into the light of day and becomes bloodily topical. This happened on a vast scale, in the lifetime of our own generation. No sooner was Hitler's *Machtübernahme* (assumption of power) a fact than the church was forced to choose its battle-front. Some churches avoided the issue in a cautious neutrality; others ventured to take action. And the spectacle of the church's attitude towards the Jews under the Nazi régime still causes a great division of opinion.

As long as eighteen years after the collapse of Germany a chance event caused the discussion to flare up again. The German author, Rolf Hochhuth, was only fourteen years old when the war ended. So he belongs to a new generation and can look with fresh eyes at the drama his parents' generation was responsible for. In 1963 theatres in many countries put on his play *Der Stellvertreter* (The Representative). The title alludes to the fact that the Pope is the Vicar (or Representative) of Christ. And it is Pius XII, Pope while the war raged, whom the play subjects to caustic criticism. As a work of art *Der Stellvertreter* does not rank very high. Its characters lack life. They are like cardboard figures, expressing conflicting ideas about the problem Hochhuth brings up for discussion: why did not Pius XII raise his voice and publicly and solemnly condemn Nazism's monstrous genocide of six million Jews? The Pope was asked to speak. Insistently, over and over again. But he remained silent. Even in the days when the Germans, literally under the Vatican's windows, put hundreds of Roman Jews in transports bound for Auschwitz.

The play was the sensation of the year. Orthodox Catholics protested in startled indignation against the criticism of His Holiness. The play was banned in Rome; in other towns there were disturbances during the performance. This insignificant play exposed a problem that had been whispered about in corners and was now suddenly put forward as a topical subject for discussion. Once again people saw that little strokes can fell great oaks. Pope Pius XII was exposed to the limelight and cut a poor figure. But what are the facts behind Hochhuth's bitter drama?

No one doubts Pope Pius's good will to the Jews in their misfortune. He showed it by his actions, unlocking the Vatican's doors and hiding many of them. He had sacred vessels melted down to ransom imprisoned Jews with the proceeds; he allowed the issue of false certificates of baptism. But however well-meaning all these things were, they were only half measures. When it came to the decisive test, the Pope failed. He was silent when he could have spoken and ought to have done so. It makes a painful impression to read the satisfied report Germany's Ambassador to the Vatican, Ernst von Weizsäcker, sent the Ministry for Foreign Affairs in Berlin after the deportation of the Jews:

'Although pressed from all sides the Pope refused to be drawn into any kind of demonstration against the deportations.'

The distinguished English historian, Hugh Trevor-Roper, who has specialised in the Nazi period, claims that the Pope's silence is at least partly explained by his political outlook. The Catholic church has always been an avowed opponent of Communism. Understandably enough, for Catholicism and Communism in their demand for obedience and discipline are of a piece, only under opposite standards and therefore mutually hostile to each other. Even if the Pope never sympathised with Nazism's activities during the war, he preferred its authoritative form of government to Communism's as the lesser of two evils. As early as the twenties the Holy See encouraged the establishment of Nazi and Fascist rule in Germany and Italy, naturally without being aware of the bestial forces that were let loose. In the years between 1917 and 1929 Pius was Papal Nuncio in Germany and in 1940 he confided to von Ribbentrop, then German Minister for Foreign Affairs, that those twelve years had been the happiest of his life. He was called 'the German Pope'; his secretary was German; the language of the papal household was German. In the summer of 1943 the papal 'Minister for Foreign Affairs' declared that Europe's future depended on a German victory on the eastern front. In this fight for life and death the Pope could not openly take sides against Germany. Of course the Pope was placed on the horns of a painful dilemma when he saw Hitler proceed to *'Die Endlosung der jüdischen Frage'*, that was to put a full stop to Jewish existence in Europe. The Pope helped the Jews in secret, but officially he was neutral and kept silent. The choice had been agonisingly difficult. But there were considerations that forced the scales down on the side of silence. The Pope did not want to create conflicts of conscience for the millions of Catholics who were soldiers in the German army. He was afraid of reprisals and believed that it was useless to influence Hitler. As far as the last point is concerned, experience in Denmark points in the opposite direction. When the Germans tried to arrest the Danish Jews, all the country's authorities and organisations protested publicly and loudly. I remember morning service in my church on the first Sunday in October 1943. Scarcely had I begun to read out the Danish bishops' fiery protest against the persecution of the Jews when the congregation rose to their feet and, after the reading, a strong unanimous amen rang through the church. One of the puzzles of the war is the 4-500 Danish Jews whom the Germans managed to take to Theresienstadt. Most of them survived and returned home. Thousands of Jews from other countries were transported to Auschwitz. But not a single Danish Jew. Why? The only answer I can give is that the Germans knew that a whole people, from the king to the humblest man in the kingdom, stood behind them and demanded that they should be sent home.

In his list of human weaknesses Dante reserves a special place in the *Divine Comedy* for the man who chose to be neutral in a great crisis. Pius XII is in that category. His silence makes him co-responsible for genocide. And if the Pope had spoken and taken the consequences, he would have raised his church to a position higher than it had ever reached in its two-thousand-year-old history.

In 1960 a group of more than a hundred American Jews had an audience of Pope John XXIII. They got into conversation and the Americans thanked him because, during the last great war, as the Vatican's apostolic delegate to Turkey and Greece, the Pope—he was Cardinal Roncalli at the time—had intervened with the Turkish authorities and guaranteed a shipload of Jewish refugees from German-occupied countries asylum in Turkey. When the Pope greeted the Jews, his words were as follows:

'When I see you before me, I think of Joseph, who for a long time kept from his brothers who he really was, but finally could not restrain his emotion. Today I feel like him and burst out:

' "You are my brothers." '

John XXIII was loved all over the world. In Italy he is called '*Il papa simpatico*' for his warmheartedness, his charming smile and not least for the courage with which he set about reforming his church. And in the scene with the American Jews we glimpse the breakthrough of something entirely new in the Roman church.

With Pope John the feeling of brotherhood with the Jews, as he expressed it here, was not an isolated feature or one inspired by the mood of the moment. Throughout his long life this view of the relationship between synagogue and church ripened and produced beautiful flowers. His help to the Jews during the war is only one of many examples. When Roncalli became Pope John, he tried to create a new feeling between the Vatican and the Jewish people in many fields. Soon a change in the otherwise chilly relations between the Vatican and the state of Israel was noticed. The encyclical 'Peace on Earth' condemned racial and religious persecution. For centuries the Good Friday prayer in Catholic churches went: *Oremus pro perfidis Judaeis*, let us pray for the perfidious Jews. When the prayer was first composed, the word *perfidis* simply meant unbelieving. At the time no Jew took offence at it. On the contrary, he was proud of being an infidel in the church's eyes. But in the course of time the word came to mean treacherous or cunning, and it corrupted the mind of the man who said the prayer. A devout Catholic had the church's authority behind him when he looked down on the treacherous Jews. Pope John ordered the offensive words

M

to be removed from the prayer and reformed other prayers of the same tenor.

So he took energetic measures against antisemitic tendencies in the church. Of course John XXIII was not the first to take such a step. To name one example, Pope Pius XI told some Belgian pilgrims in 1938 that 'antisemitism is a movement we Christians cannot have any part in; spiritually speaking we are all Semites'. And the truth is, and every Christian should know it, that antisemitism is antitheism, it is turned against God. But deep in the mind, engraved on the unconscious, taught by church and school for countless ages, lurks the accusation against the Jews that they murdered Christ and that all generations of Israel are responsible for this action. Until this point is settled, there is no hope for frank conversations, for trust and brotherhood between Jews and Christians. It was Pope John's historic task to set forces in motion to pluck this poisonous growth up by the roots.

In an inspired moment he decided to convene the great council in Rome and gave the ageing German Jesuit Augustin Bea the task of including in the document on Christian unity the church's official condemnation of the charge against the Jews of murdering Christ. But the treatment of this problem had a difficult passage through the council's complicated channels of procedure. It was hampered by intrigues and obstructed by massive resistance on the part of the Curia's arch-conservative minority and met with open hostility from princes of the church in Arab countries, who declared that the resolution took the State of Israel's side.

The matter was not made any easier by the death of Pope John shortly after the council ended its first session. His successor Paul VI is cautious where John was bold, a cold reflective nature in contrast with his predecessor's spontaneous warm-heartedness and intuitive way of grasping the nettle. The present Pope has not had the same background as John XXIII in his relations with the Jews, either. Montini, as he was then called, was one of the Vatican's Secretaries of State during the war and in that capacity conducted the difficult negotiations with the German ambassador in 1943. Consequently, he was involved in, and co-responsible for, the Pope's notorious silence about the extermination of Europe's Jews. Perhaps it was a lapse when Montini, as archbishop of Milan in 1958, wrote an approving introduction to an anti-semitic book, however compromising it may sound. But it must be admitted that he continued Pope John's line in the council and backed up Cardinal Bea in his efforts to pilot the document outlining the church's new view of the Jews into harbour on its difficult voyage between hidden rocks and dangerous whirlpools.

At last the council reached its goal in the autumn of 1965. However, the result was not so brilliantly clear as people might have expected after Pope John's careful preparations. Admittedly, the proclamation recognises the church's debt to, and respect for, Israel, and declares that what happened to Christ in his suffering cannot be laid at the door of all Jews who lived then or Jews today, and therefore lays down that no one when catechising or preaching shall represent the Jews as rejected or cursed by God, as if the council deplores antisemitic hate and persecution. But condemnation of the word *deicidii*, deicides, dropped out of the last draft of the document and the expression that the council 'condemns' antisemitism was modified to 'deplores'.

Nevertheless, the declaration is a milestone in the church's attitude towards the Jews. If its provisions are actually carried out throughout the world, it will mean a radical purification of Christian preaching in Catholic schools and pulpits. It will take time for the fruit to ripen, but the first step towards a new future has been taken.

Yet the fact that it cost such tremendous efforts for 2,500 intelligent and highly educated men to reach a result which an outsider considers a foregone conclusion, illustrates how the church was still enveloped in age-old prejudice. And we understand the sardonic wit shown by a Jewish journalist in connection with the council's belated result, when he recommended that a Jewish council should be convened without delay to deal with a document about the church's debt to the Jews and forgive the persecutions of the Crusades, the Inquisition, the ghetto and the expulsions, and declare the Christians who are alive today innocent of, and not responsible for, the crimes their fathers committed against the Jews in days gone by! Or another Jewish writer who bitterly pointed out that the council concerned itself solely with Jesus's death and passed lightly over what happened to the Jews in Europe during the war. After all, that involved six million dead in our own day, but there was only one man who died 2,000 years ago!

14 / DIALOGUE

SUMMER SUN OVER BARCELONA, THE
capital of the kingdom of Catalonia, one July
day 700 years ago. Above the spires and towers
of the royal palace long embroidered banners waved in a fresh
breeze from the sea. A brilliant play was about to be performed. The scene teemed with courtiers and knights in red,
yellow and blue silk garments; their jewel-encrusted weapons
clanked. It looked like the scene at a medieval tournament
when bold warriors challenged one another to joust to the
death and the victor accepted the prize from the hand of the
most beautiful lady. But the tournament on this day was
not fought with lances and swords; ideas and words were
splintered here. A solemn psalm-singing procession of ecclesi-
astics emerged between the elegant knights; it was the archbishop with his entourage of priests and learned theologians.
Their opponents were not very conspicuous in the glittering
assembly. They were a crowd of black-clad Jewish rabbis with
an old scholar at their head, the celebrated Moses ben Nach-
man, also called Nachmanides. A summons from King James
of Catalonia had torn him away from a peaceful life in
Gerona where he had worked until his seventieth year, surrounded by his family and many pupils. He was one side in
the 'Tournament for God and the Faith' which the king
called the 'disputation'. Nachmanides was to fight with the
church's Brother, Pablo Christiani, to decide which religion
was the true one, the synagogue's or the church's.

The result was a foregone conclusion. The church had

the power and it had to conquer. But arguing with Jews has never been such a simple matter. They have always been exiles and defenceless. However, nature teaches the weak to defend themselves and develop the qualities they need. The Jews learned diplomacy and ingenuity; they became more worldly wise than their enemies. Not for nothing had their intelligence been sharpened on the Talmud's whetstone from time immemorial; they became swift and surprisingly subtle in their replies.

The tournament at Barcelona lasted for four days. It is the most famous of many in which the church challenged the synagogue to controversy. But every time the Jews surprised their adversaries. In this intellectual game of chess, everything was at stake if they lost. But neither did they dare to win outright. Both results would be fatal. So they did not checkmate their opponent, even if they could have done so, but tried for a draw. It required strong nerves to balance on the sharp edge when they apparently let the church win, but never gave up their own rights. Scholarship, boldness and dexterous tricks—all were called for.

Nachmanides faced a renegade Jew. In these discussions the church used the very men who had been brought up in Judaism but for one reason or another had suffered spiritual shipwreck and gone over to the church. They knew the Talmud from within and brought to light points which could be interpreted as blasphemous or slanderous to Christian dogma. Brother Pablo was accustomed to shining when he proved truths of the Christian faith from the Talmud. His brothers in the same order looked on him as a chosen tool for converting Jews.

Both sides had armed themselves. On both Christian and Jewish sides learned theologians wrote handbooks in which arguments and questions and answers were systematically arranged and easy to find when they were needed in the heat of battle. Some of these guides still exist, so that we can follow the discussions at close quarters. The Jews naturally found points to attack in the Christian doctrine of the Trinity and God's Mother. They also asked to whom Jesus had called on the cross, when he complained: 'My God, my God, why hast thou forsaken me?' Was he asking himself for help, for after all he was God? And why had he not come four thousand years before he did come, to free mankind from the original sin stemming from Adam and Eve? Then he would have made hundreds of generations happy, who now had to suffer all the torments of purgatory. And—the argument went on—how can you Christians claim that the Jews are scattered all over the world as a punishment because their forefathers abandoned Christ to suffering and death? If Jesus came to earth to redeem men by his death, the ancient Jews were only acting in his spirit by letting him die. Why should their descendants be punished? Looking at it fairly they had done a good deed.

The subjects under discussion at Barcelona were the usual ones when Jews and Christians debated their faith. Had the Messiah already come or were people to await him? Was he born of Jewish parents or was he of divine nature? Nachmanides claimed that the prophets had foretold that the Messiah would usher in an era of peace, but that it had not come yet.

'It is written that the peoples shall beat their swords into ploughshares and no one shall learn war any more. What if you, O King, and your knights were forced to put your art of fencing on the shelf already?'

The climax came when Nachmanides turned directly to the king and burst out:

'Thou, Lord King, art son of a Christian man and born of a Christian woman. All thy life Christian priests have hammered one thing home into thy mind, an idea that is absolutely contrary to everything that reason, nature and the prophets tell us: that the creator of heaven and earth should become flesh and blood in a Jewish woman's womb, undergo a normal pregnancy, be born as an infant, grow up and be handed over to his enemies, condemned to death, executed and finally rise again from the dead to return to his divine condition. Such ideas are unintelligible to us Jews. All your rhetoric is vain. On this point our ways part, never to meet again!'

In the middle of the argument Nachmanides scored a point with his ready wit. Brother Pablo said that the doctrine of the Trinity was so deep a mystery that not even the angels could fathom it. In a flash Nachmanides retorted:

'In that case you can scarcely blame us for finding this mystery incomprehensible too!'

There are flashes in these discussions from olden days that are topical to this very day in conflicts between the two religions. But Nachmanides' bold speech caused irritation, and he suggested that the king stop the disputation after four days had past. The king agreed to this and incidentally paid Nachmanides many compliments as well. He said that he had never heard such a brilliant defence of an unjust cause. But the inevitable result was that the church proclaimed its victory. For safety's sake the monks drove Nachmanides out of the country. He went to Palestine and spent his last years there.

The disputation at Barcelona stands as an object lesson in how the powerful overcomes the weak and tries to force an unbeliever to see the true light. If he cannot reach his goal by the weight of his arguments, he uses force. Another disputation at Paris ended with twenty-four waggonloads of Talmudic writings being ceremoniously burnt at the stake. The last of the medieval disputations took place in 1413 or 1414 at Tortosa. It lasted for one year and nine months and was attended by the pope himself. These intellectual tournaments were the forerunners of the Inquisition. That ecclesiastical court definitively reduced the opposition to silence. The rack and the stake stifled the last answer the Jews could gasp out:

'Hear O Israel, the Lord our God is one.'

When the autos-da-fé were over and the fires at the stake burnt out, the church held the floor without contradiction. There was no question of a dialogue here, only monologue. For dialogue is conversation, monologue soliloquy.

Centuries were to pass before synagogue and church met on an equal footing and tried their strength in freedom and mutual respect. The road led from conflict to conversation. We find the first sign of this new relationship in the 1750's with the friendship between Ephraim Gotthold Lessing and Moses Mendelssohn, and the latter's debate with Johann Caspar Lavater. Only then did men begin to grasp what lies in the precious word 'tolerance' and the monologue at last become a dialogue.

Moses Mendelssohn was the first of a new Jewish type. As a weak hunchbacked lad of fourteen from the ghetto in Dessau he walked the long windy road to Berlin, where he educated himself in poverty. It was the old story of a man having to go through a great deal to become famous. But he was rewarded by finally becoming one of the age's most respected philosophers. Mendelssohn's achievement was to break a hole in the ghetto wall from within and lead his people out among other men. The fact that many Jews were blinded by the sun's bright light and could not find their way as soon as they escaped from the semi-darkness of confinement is another story. In their uncontrollable urge to reach the world outside, many of them bought a new future at the cost of faithlessness to their inherited tradition. Old bonds snapped like thread; there was mass apostasy from Judaism. Emancipation was followed by assimilation, that is to say absorption by the community outside the ghetto. It was the most serious crisis which the Jewish people had ever faced, and to this very day it is fighting to escape from it alive.

We shall soon see how young generations are turning back to the old paths and finding new fresh expressions of their traditional faith and are also able to meet the church on a brand-new footing. The tree has shown itself vigorous enough to put out new shoots where withered branches have dropped off.

Moses Mendelssohn inspired his friend Lessing to write the play *Nathan der Weise* and is himself portrayed as its main character, the Jew Nathan. The drama plays on the story of the three rings in the Decameron. Lessing represents the three great religions, Judaism, Christianity and Islam, by three brothers, each of whom claims that *he* owns the original ring. They stand for the three religions' rivalry as to which of them is the one true religion. The point of the play is that the three brothers' rings can be equally genuine—and equally false. For religions are attempts to comprehend the incomprehensible. But only an attempt. Therefore the differences between them are unimportant in comparison with the humanity and morality they aim at creating, and when this is understood, mutual tolerance is born. What was epoch-making was the boldness with which Lessing made Nathan the drama's central figure, in brilliant contrast to the Shakespearian Shylock. That had not been seen before. A new era in the relationship between synagogue and church had been introduced.

Moses Mendelssohn remained loyal to his Jewish faith. He observed its commandments with scrupulous care and kept his permanent seat in the synagogue. His aim was never to step into the foreground and attract attention; on the contrary he preferred to keep in the background. However, he was not allowed to sit in his own quiet corner. Instead he was whirled into a debate which was followed closely by the whole of Europe. Johann Caspar Lavater, the eccentric clergyman from Zurich, the Christian counterpart of the authors of the *Sturm und Drang* period, was zealous, indeed fanatical, in his drive to proclaim his faith to unbelievers. He tried his hand at it with everyone he met, including Goethe and Rousseau. Lavater was a genuine admirer of Mendelssohn and could not understand that so noble a person was a stranger to Christianity. Driven by his impulsive mind, he publicly challenged Mendelssohn to refute Christianity or to draw the obvious conclusion and allow himself to be baptised.

Mendelssohn was upset by the challenge. He had never

believed in the value of discussions and it went against his peaceable nature to clash with people who thought differently. But he accepted the challenge and answered. His answer gave rise to fresh arguments and a swarm of articles, and pamphlets flooded Europe for years.

Mendelssohn was a child of his time, the *leitmotiv* of which consisted of words such as enlightenment and reason. So it was only natural for him to see Judaism's advantage over Christianity in its reasonableness. It was free of dogmas based on faith that went beyond reason. And reason forced him to reject Christian dogmas such as the Trinity, incarnation and Christ's death as the Redeemer. The difference between the Old and the New Testaments was that the former was in harmony with reason or at least did not conflict with it, whereas the latter called for a faith that reason could not acknowledge. Of course, Mendelssohn asserted that his Jewish faith was a revelation from God, but said that rational thinking was bound to lead others to recognise its truth.

There is a sentence in the Talmud that bears witness to Jewish tolerance: 'The righteous of all faiths have a share in the world to come'. Mendelssohn quoted it and based his attitude on it. Not out of indifference to his own people, or because Judaism and Christianity grew up from the same roots, but from his faith in human fellowship.

Mendelssohn did not penetrate very deeply in his examination of religion. The further one follows the long debate, the clearer that becomes. He forgets the essence of the Jewish faith, that God is alive, that He acts in a sovereign way, intervenes in His people's history and reveals not only the law but also dogmas, for example that He created the world from nothing. But in his religious superficiality Mendelssohn is on a par with his Christian partners, because he was a child of the age of enlightenment and was unable to perceive the heart-beat in genuine belief in God.

However, the innovation in the debate between Mendelssohn and Lavater, and all the discussions that followed in its wake, was that now Jew and Christian met in conversation. For the first time in the long common history of Israel and the church we witness a well-meant attempt by both sides to understand, tolerate and respect each other. Jews and Christians dealt seriously with the problems and discussed the differences that separated the two religions, and recognised that both of them could have a share in the ultimate unique truth. Without denying or concealing serious divergencies, they met on common human ground. It is significant to read one of Mendelssohn's letters to Herder which begins: 'Moses the man writes to Herder the man and not the Jew to the Christian'. Never mind that the ideas on both sides are disastrously abbreviated and foolish; that was inherent in the chill intellectual atmosphere of the age. The very fact that Jew is talking to Christian, that we are listening to a dialogue, is a milestone. It is as if we had been transported to another world from the one in which the medieval disputations took place. Everything points the way to new perspectives.

A dialogue is not a one-way street. Nor is it a game of tennis in which what matters is that I am alert and quick, so that every time the ball sails over the net into my half of the court, it is hit back, preferably so hard that my opponent cannot return it. But many conversations take just that form. Each person thinks only of what he is saying and only listens to the other in order to contradict him. In such cases the conversation is not a dialogue, but narrows down to two monologues, and the result is that both sides remain more firmly convinced of their own viewpoint than before they met.

The medieval disputations were such double monologues. Jews and Christians were not partners but opponents, and great matters were at stake for both of them. The church had to defend and increase its prestige, the Jews thought only of saving their skins. Neither of them listened in order to understand the other, and neither dared to be receptive to fact that there might be a glimpse of truth in what the other said. But the secret of a real dialogue is precisely that each of the two participants listens and manages to see his own conviction through the other's eyes. It is more profitable than simply showing oneself to be right and the other wrong.

The prerequisite is, of course, that both can speak in freedom and not risk their lives if one of them happens to reveal himself a heretic or is caught out in blasphemy. And the Jews of old in Barcelona and Paris and Tortosa did not have such freedom. For that matter neither did Mendelssohn have it. But Mendelssohn knew that he had to be discreet and express himself carefully. In the Germany of those days the Jews' welfare hung on a thin thread. At any moment some prince might feel insulted and drive Mendelssohn out of Berlin or expel his brothers from one of the many German States. External freedom is a condition of inner freedom. Freedom of belief and speech are benefits that were not won until our time. And even now we must not feel too certain that we possess them as completely as we are supposed to, or that they are guaranteed us for ever.

In an age when everyone resembles his neighbour more and more, it may sound strange when the writer claims that on the contrary one of life's riches lies hidden in the fact that we are different and that conformity makes life flat and colourless, even when religion is in question. There are people who assert that all religions really say the same thing and therefore are one. What matters is to find and hold on to what is common to them. However, there are greater values in the differences between them, and the uniqueness, that which gives Judaism and Christianity their special stamp, must never be sacrificed to enforcing a superficial and feeble unity. Different as the two sister religions are and however deep a gulf gapes between them, neither of them, when Jew and Christian meet in dialogue, must give up a grain of conviction.

But if there is to be any benefit from the meeting of Jew and Christian, he who has always dominated must be ready to admit the injustice he has done the other. The only chance of the Jews' forgetting the church's debt to them lies in the church never forgetting it. It was in Jesus's name that the Jews were persecuted and massacred for thousands of years; in his name they were forcibly baptised and their children were taken from them and put into monasteries. The church, on the contrary, has never been persecuted in Sinai's or the Torah's name. For us Christians one man was crucified, but Jewish history has been one long and constant crucifixion.

So the church must take the first step; it must hold out its hand and beg forgiveness. And it must renounce its stiff self-assurance and feeling of superiority and monopoly of the revelation and listen to what its elder sister has to say from its age-old loyalty to its fathers' faith. It is not for me but for its own men to say that the synagogue for its part must learn to see the church with new eyes. The main thing is to understand that it has certainly been a puzzle to the church that Israel was, and is, blind to Christ, but it is just as deep a tragedy that the church is blind to Israel.

Dialogue begins with listening to and understanding one another.

During the First World War two young German Jews lay in their trenches, one on the Macedonian, the other on the French front. Franz Rosenzweig belonged to the synagogue; Eugen Rosenstock had been baptised into the church out of deep conviction. Their exchange of letters between holes in the trenches is a fine example of dialogue between Jew and Christian. For Franz Rosenzweig the result of the ideas that were born of listening to a Christian friend became a book that tells Christians how a modern Jew can experience his fathers' faith and form a new view of it and its relation to the church's faith. We shall follow Rosenzweig's life and ideas—and listen to them.

The Rosenzweigs were an old Jewish family with roots back in a German *Judengasse*. But around the turn of the last century they had become as assimilated as Jews can be without actually joining the church. Franz Rosenzweig once teased his mother by saying that the only Jewish word he knew from home was *rishes* (literally wicked), the Yiddish for antisemitism. It always clung to German Jews, both in secret and openly, however much they tried to become as German as the Germans themselves, or preferably more so. His home was at Kassel, his father a prosperous manufacturer of dye-stuffs. Franz Rosenzweig was born in 1886. He left school at the age of eighteen with excellent marks and was considered an exceptionally gifted person. And we have the picture of a young student coming from a rich and assimilated Jewish background, something of a genius, with enough money to pursue whatever studies might interest him. He went to the best universities of the day, alternated between different branches of study and had a wide range of interests. That did not mean that he was one of those who know a little about everything. In our time no one has time or money to broaden his studies. One has to concentrate, become expert in a single field, know a lot about a little. But when Rosenzweig was young, there were still people living who managed to become what a vanished age saw as the ideal of the intellectual: a polymath to whom nothing human was foreign. In his works Rosenzweig showed that he belonged to the last generation of that proud race.

In the midst of these swarming interests the scattered golden remnants of Judaism that he brought with him from his childhood faded and he advanced towards the crisis in his life. It came in 1913. At the University of Leipzig he had made friends with Eugen Rosenstock, a brilliant young man, even more erudite than himself, who had gone over to Christianity. In his early enthusiasm for his new faith he saw it as his duty to act as missionary among other Jews. His first task was to win Franz Rosenzweig. And suddenly the latter found himself under powerful pressure, both personal and intellectual. He desperately lacked weapons to defend himself with. His Jewish inheritance was an anachronism or at best a rudiment. What was more, it was incapable of convincing modern men. Only one way remained open, to turn to the religion of the West and become a Christian.

One summer evening Rosenzweig gave up in the face of his friend's arguments and decided to have himself baptised. But on one condition. He would join the church in the same way as those who founded it in their day, as a Jew, not a heathen. By that he meant that Christianity was the further development of a Judaism that was inadequate.

So in the autumn of 1913 he continued to attend the synagogue services on the main holy-days—the Jewish New Year and Yom Kippur, the Day of Atonement—before he applied to join the church. At home in Kassel he went to the New Year's Day service without it making an impression on him. Later he was in Berlin, and on the night before Yom Kippur, went to the service in a humble synagogue in a side street.

But something unexpected happened during the service.

Yom Kippur, the Day of Atonement, is the climax of the Jewish year. On that day the Jew stands alone before God, wrapped in his prayer shawl as at the hour of his death. Here the Jew is the man, God the world's judge. The drama begins the night before, for the Jewish day runs from sunset to sunset. Before he enters the synagogue, the Jew must have settled all disputes with his neighbours and asked for forgiveness. Then, it is solely a question of his debt to God. The evening service is called Kol Nidre; the words mean 'all vows', after the prayer for forgiveness for promises to God that were not kept. The next day the liturgy at the morning, Musaph (additional) and afternoon services begins with psalms and reading of the scriptures. The Musaph service includes a reminiscence of the temple ritual of the past in which the high priest pronounced God's ineffable name for the only time in the year, and the day reaches its conclusion when the ram's horn, the *shofar*, sounds through the hall.

Franz Rosenzweig left the synagogue like a new man. He had believed that the church was the place where modern man could find a faith that created harmony out of chaos. But that was precisely what he had experienced in the synagogue.

At the very moment that he intended to leave his fathers' faith, he awoke to see that Judaism was the way for him. How it happened we do not know; he never spoke about it. Here was holy ground, a secret between the otherwise so frank and eloquent Rosenzweig and God. But everyone noticed that he had lived through a decisive crisis.

The next year was 1914. The Great War broke out and Rosenzweig joined the colours as a volunteer. For he was German and wanted to do his duty. Rosenzweig served in an anti-aircraft unit on the Macedonian front. For the majority of soldiers life in the trenches was a grey, monotonous and miserable existence of perpetual struggle against mud and deadly perils. It was different for Rosenzweig. His restless inquiring mind never left him in peace. As often as his duties allowed, he sat absorbed in his books or wrote letters and treatises. His great experience was his encounter with Polish Judaism. Rosenzweig was stationed in Warsaw for a time, and there he saw Judaism in full flower with schools, Talmudic academies and lively services with singing. He listened to the sound of the voices, in which young blended with old, and he wrote home that he had never heard people pray as they did here. It was as if these living breathing Jewish masses tore a veil from his eyes and showed the gulf between real Judaism and the Philistine Jews of the German bourgeoisie among whom he had grown up. This new discovery of the primal masses of the Jewish people worked like a blood transfusion on Rosenzweig's mind, and the picture of the Polish Jews became the yardstick by which he later measured the undeniably stunted Jewish life at home in Germany.

When the war drew to an end and the Macedonian front collapsed, this incredibly vital young man began to write his major work, *Der Stern der Erlösung*, The Star of the Redemption. The book was written when he was under fire or waiting for battle, in field hospitals, wounded, ill with malaria, ravaged by influenza (it was the period of the Spanish variety), once so ill that he lay in a coma for three days, and during the dramatic retreat through the Balkans after Germany's

N

collapse. On top of that, it was written on hastily composed postcards which he sent to his mother, who had fair copies made of them. Even under normal conditions the creation of such a work in a short time would have been an achievement, but written in the desperate circumstances that were the lot of a soldier in the front line of a defeated army, it was simply fantastic. This difficult book testifies to the author's wide reading and deep familiarity with classical Judaism. It is the first grandiose attempt to create a synthesis of faith and knowledge that modern Jews can live and die by.

While Franz Rosenzweig lay at his observation post outside Salonika, it dawned on him where his mission in life lay. His literary activity was to be sporadic; more important than books was a college where he and like-minded men could lead German Jews back from the verge of the abyss on which they lived to the centre of the Jewish faith. Immediately after the war he succeeded in realising his idea with an academy at Frankfurt. There he worked together with a circle of outstanding teachers, among whom was Martin Buber. The academy had a brilliant start and became one of the factors that gave the German Jews strength to perish with moral dignity in the hell of Nazism.

But at the very height of his career Rosenzweig was smitten with a fatal illness, a form of sclerosis that partially crippled him. During his last eight years he sat totally crippled, tied tightly to a specially constructed chair, and finally he became dumb. But he did not give up; his invalid chair became a centre of Jewish religious and intellectual activity. His wife read from his look what he wanted written down. He dictated letters and treatises. He kept his sense of humour and deprecated sympathy; self-pity was unknown to him. Visitors were moved by the sight of this rare victory of mind over matter. He lived with the cheerfulness in adversity that a man only wins who is face to face with the Almighty.

Franz Rosenzweig died in 1929. He was forty-three.

His youthful discussions with Eugen Rosenstock already

show that Franz Rosenzweig took up problems and boldly ventured to consider them with a fresh eye. It was something new when a Jew claimed that his people's history and faith had to be seen in relation to Christianity and compared with it. Judaism and Christianity are, he says, mutually dependent on each other, and the one supplements the other. The title of his major book is *The Star of the Redemption* and the image in it of a shining star, or more accurately a sun, symbolises both the religions.

Judaism first. It is the fire in the sun, but it remains in the sun and never moves away from it. It remains where God lit it when the covenant was made at Sinai; there it is inviolable and out of the range of any interference by history. For it possesses everything that is worth possessing. Judaism's first duty is to continue to be itself and never change. To the Jew religion is not something added to his personality or introduced from without. It is not a part of him, but is his very being. The Jew is a Jew; he is born a Jew; he is simply Faith itself and possesses God by virtue of being a part of Israel. That is the reason why dogmas and creeds play so little part in Judaism; they are simply superfluous. Outside Israel, Jesus's words from the Gospel according to St. John hold good: 'No man cometh unto the Father but by me.' But, says Rosenzweig, note that he says 'cometh'. It is quite different for the man who does not need to *come*, but already *is* with the Father.

Next Christianity. As Judaism is the fire in the sun, Christianity is its rays. If Judaism had been God's only covenant with men, the rest of the world would never have been redeemed. Judaism must remain self-contained and not venture outside. Therefore God made yet another covenant, the covenant on Golgotha, which created Christianity. God wants the whole world to be redeemed, so He lets Christianity's rays shine on those who do not possess God from birth, but need to find and win Him. The Christian is different from the Jew; he is not born a Christian, but he becomes one. He is of heathen origin and must strive to become a Christian. Faith

makes him become one. He has to be converted from his in-
nate heathenism to become a Christian.

Such are the two ways to God, one for the born Jew, the
other for everyone else. Neither of the two religions possesses
the absolute truth; they are both human understandings of
the divine truth. But the ultimate and complete truth will
be revealed only when God finally comes. On that day God
will become all things to all men; the two ways will run together and be united. This will happen in the Messianic
kingdom. On that day God's name will become One. Until
then the two ways run separately; each of them does the work
imposed on them by their destiny. The ultimate recognition
is that God alone is Truth. It is God that is Truth, not Truth
that is God. For God is greater than Truth.

When Rosenzweig puts the two covenants side by side
like that, it would seem obvious to think that they are equal
and have the same value. Of course Rosenzweig does not
mean that; such liberalism would be indifference to his own
people. Men can become so tolerant towards the opinions and
faith of others that they forget to emphasise the values that
are entrusted to them. In such cases everything is blurred.
And since Rosenzweig is a Jew to the depths of his being
and on top of that one of the century's clearest existentialist
thinkers, he draws in the frontiers so that they cannot be
misinterpreted.

True enough, he gives Christianity an important place
in God's government of the world, but it is subordinate to
Judaism. That is already implicit in the fact that Judaism is
the older. Rosenzweig uses the misleading image of Judaism
as the mother and Christianity as the daughter. Admittedly
neither is Judaism the ultimate truth, but it stands nearer
to it than any other religion, including Christianity. Christianity's task is to pave the way for the Messiah. But at the
end of time the 'Son' shall cease to be Lord; then God shall
be all things to all men.

And Rosenzweig goes further. He emphasises the dangers he finds the Christian drifting into. He began as a

heathen and always carries the heathen in his heart and is tempted to yield to him. Because of this ingrained heathen urge the Christian needs a God who is a man. That is why he believes in Jesus. But one-sided devotion to the Son makes him forget the Father; he comes close to turning the second figure in the Trinity into a heathen god. Judaism must help the Christian to overcome this temptation.

The final result of Rosenzweig's reflections on the relationship between Judaism and Christianity can be summed up in his own words:

'Before God there are two, the Jew and the Christian, workers on a common task. He cannot do without either of them. He has made them eternal enemies and at the same time entwined their paths and interwoven them in the most intimate way.'

The dialogue between synagogue and church has lasted as long as synagogue and church have existed. But until modern times the dialogue between the two had never been genuine. It had consisted of two monologues in which neither side listened with an open mind to what the other had to say. The turning point came two hundred years ago. From Moses Mendelssohn's day the tone changed and the two former enemies began to exchange ideas on an equal footing. But the breakthrough to real dialogue only came with Franz Rosenzweig and then only from the synagogue's side. It can safely be said that Rosenzweig takes Christianity's spiritual claims more seriously than any Christian has taken Judaism's.

But a development is under way. Currents are awakening in the church that are discovering Judaism's values, and some clergymen are beginning to wonder if the church is not becoming impoverished by being deaf and blind to God's faithfulness to the people with whom his first covenant was made. And wide circles in the Christian world were suddenly startled into attention when the Jewish people won back its ancient country and a world was the astonished witness to the return home of hundreds of thousands of exiled Jews.

We began this book by establishing the fact that the Jewish people has survived against all expectation. We cannot conclude it until the second fact is placed beside the first one, namely that the Jewish state of Israel now exists. For facts will sooner or later show themselves stronger than inherited prejudices and stubborn conviction of superiority.

A LEGEND IN THE TALMUD RECOUNTS THAT one August day in the year 70, Ab 9 according to the Jewish calendar, when Titus's legions stormed Jerusalem and set fire to the holy temple, the surviving temple priests took refuge on the roof of the sanctuary. Section after section of the building collapsed under the onslaught of the flames and the priests had to retreat further and further as the fire spread. The wave of heat from the mighty pyre rolled towards them; their white robes with blue bands filled like taut sails. They grew steadily fewer as one after another was overtaken by the fire and fell stupefied into the sea of flames. Finally only the high priest was left; he stood alone on the farthest tip of the last section of the temple. When flames and smoke enveloped him, he plucked the golden key of Jerusalem from his bosom, hurled it up towards heaven and as he hurtled into the abyss he cried: 'Lord of the world, now you must guard your city yourself!' And, concludes the legend, at that moment a hand reached out from heaven, closed on the key and drew it up into the deep blue sky. Since then the key has never been seen again.

The legend has been handed down from father to son for thousands of years, but in May 1948, during the days when the Arab Legion made its decisive attack on the Jewish quarter in Jerusalem's old city, it became topical as never before. Bearded pious Jews knew something and whispered to one another that the commander-in-chief of Israel's new army had found the key in the Hurva synagogue, the most venerable of Jerusalem's old synagogues. It was a sign that the Almighty had forgotten his wrath against the Jews and finally returned the holy city to them.

Never mind if critical and short-sighted scholars shake their heads at such superstition and reject a legend like this one. Yet for countless generations it lent wings to men's imagination. In a flash it allows us to glimpse a hope that was never extinguished. And the pious Jews' revival of the legend indicates that there is something in the creation of modern Israel that goes beyond cold intellectual comprehension. They have good reason for telling of a key, a key that unlocks doors that have been locked for thousands of years. But the key also opens up perspectives for the man who sees a sign from above in an event that is more than a random constellation of factors, in which history in one of its inexplicable caprices put things to rights, so that the result was the Jewish state. Watching tensely and holding his breath, he sees God's hand with the golden key and hears the grating sound of an old rusty lock which the key is opening.

In the middle of the First World War, one day in 1915, Great Britain's ambassador in Paris was visited by the Jewish chemist, Dr. Chaim Weizmann. Weizmann was the leading Zionist politician. He was constantly travelling and working for the idea of opening up the holy land to its exiled people and giving them back their fathers' heritage. And now he sat in Paris, expounding his plans to the influential British diplomat.

The same evening the ambassador made a note of the visit in his diary. He wrote that he had witnessed a remarkable contradiction that day, a kind of mental split. He had met a man with brilliant scientific talents and an acute ability for making rational analyses, but on one single point, in his political ideas, he was unbalanced, nay insane.

However, it sometimes happens that the insane prove right after all and it is the clever who are stupid. One can believe in something impossible and disregard rational opinion concerning the possibility of realising it. And the belief conquers. For the strongest forces in life are invisible—like Jehovah in Jerusalem's temple, which was empty of images. At the right moment the intangible reality fights its way through and shows itself in visions to the man who believes, and gives him enthusiasm and strength to carry out the visions in so-called reality.

A Russian historian has said that the Slavs have no history, only geography. With the Jews it is the other way round: they have plenty of history, but no geography. Roaming the world homeless for two thousand years they never forgot Zion. Every year at the Passover the exiles greeted each other with 'Next year in Jerusalem', and their Torah commanded them to celebrate the wine harvest in the lost homeland. Disraeli was thinking of this when he said that a people that continued to celebrate the wine harvest although it had no grapes to harvest would get its vineyards back again one day. Wherever the Jew wandered, he had his roots far away, in a country that only the very few could hope to see with their own eyes.

And in the end, after interminable years of waiting, it happened. A new reality emerged from the ghetto's pale dreams and bitter tears. Right in the middle of a sober, critical and materialistic age, miracles, tangible miracles began to fall from heaven. The homeless people got its country back.

In the long history of mankind the release of the people of Israel from their bondage in Egypt has stood out as the great example of liberation from slavery. Time out of number the parting of the Red Sea has thrown sparks into despairing minds and caused fresh courage to flare up. A similar sense of wonder is associated with the birth of the new Israel in our time. Scepticism and doubt were put to shame by hope and faith. As long as there are people who fight against injustice and tyranny, this event will be remembered. The Jewish people has given the world a new gift.

Of course, the man who tries to make these events appear as the fulfilment of the Bible's prophecies is treading on thin

ice. In the Christian church we have met plenty of vision-
aries who made contemporary politics fit in with the Bible's
words and were never afraid of cutting off a heel or clipping
a toe to make the sum work out without a remainder. Nevertheless, many Christians are surprised when, in the light of
the new Israel, they read the words of the prophet Amos
saying that the Lord shall turn his people Israel's destiny
and raise David's fallen tabernacle; that they shall build the
waste cities, plant vineyards and make gardens. Or the prophet Zechariah: 'Behold, I will save my people from the east
country, and from the west country; . . . and they shall
dwell in the midst of Jerusalem.' The fact that God from
remote times has bound up the chosen people's destiny with
the holy land—*Ha'aretz* it is called, the land, with a definite
article, i.e. the only one—runs like a red thread through the
books of the Bible from the Lord's promise to Abraham to
give this country to him and his descendants. It is not surprising that Jerusalem continued to be the centre of the
world to the Jews wherever they were scattered in diaspora.
Three times in the chosen people's history it returned to
Ha'aretz, at the time of the exodus from Egypt, after the
homecoming from Babylon and in our own time. The first
two times God rewarded faith and obedience. But if we read
the prophets about the last homecoming, they say rather that
God shall give a sign, create something miraculous, that
stands as a challenge and a warning from Him. Seen in that
light Israel's re-establishment is a link in God's plan.

For the first time since the gospel from Jerusalem went
forth into the world, the synagogue in the new Israel is the
one which has the power when it meets the church. For Israel
is the Jews' country. If one wakes up early in the morning in
Jerusalem, the chiming of distant church bells is heard.
Heavy deep tones blend with light ones and dedicate the new
day to God. Before Israel became master of the whole of
Jerusalem, the bells were heard outside her borders; their
chiming rang from the old quarter of the city, behind the
barbed-wire fence that till June, 1967, cut Jerusalem into two

cities. And in Tel Aviv one must go right out into the part
of the town that once was Jaffa to hear church bells. There
are no churches anywhere else in this, the world's only
example of a purely Jewish big city. And Sunday is not
Sunday, but an ordinary weekday; the shops are open, busy
people hurry through the streets. It is the Sabbath that is
holy. And when Queen Sabbath makes her entry, all the
bustle ceases and holy peace descends on the country, for the
Sabbath characterises Israel to a greater degree than the
puritanical Sunday in England and Scotland. Time after time
the foreigner is reminded that he is visiting a Jewish country.
At the butcher's he can only buy meat that has been ritually
slaughtered. The language is the Hebrew of the Bible,
revived and brought up to date to meet modern needs. The
Bible is a subject at school, as is the history of the fatherland.
Men with long sidelocks walk through the streets, for it says
in the Torah that 'Thou shalt not trim thy hair at the
temples', and during mealtimes many men wear the little flat
skullcap that marks an orthodox Jew.

Of course, it can be debated how deeply Jewish faith is
implanted in Israel's people, but it is not easy to check this,
and judgment depends on one's own attitude and more or less
random impressions. There are circles in Europe and
America which are fond of asserting that the people of Israel
have broken away from religious life, and that religion there
is reduced to seeking shelter in small isolated enclaves, which
become smaller and smaller as the rising generations abandon
the faith of their childhood. And it is true that there are
some, even wide circles in Israel that are remote from the
religion of their forefathers. How should the people of Israel
remain unaffected by the wave of secularisation that has swept
across the world since the days of the Renaissance? Yet it is
my impression that its effects have been less pronounced in
Israel than in most other countries where I have had the
opportunity to follow this development at first hand.

'We call the country *Eretz Yisrael*, which means "the
Land of Israel". And if we scratch only a little way into the

ground we find Israel.' It was the late Moshe Sharett, once Israel's Prime Minister and Minister for Foreign Affairs, who said this to me during a conversation. He meant to emphasise wittily how archaeological investigations in Palestine repeatedly demonstrate that it was once the land of the Jews. But the words apply not only to the country; they are also true of the mentality of its people. Anyone who delves beneath the surface finds imperishable signs that it has been ploughed with the plough of religion for millennia. It will take more than a generation or two to eradicate them. If it ever happens.

The Jews say Ha'aretz when they think of Palestine, but Christians speak of the Holy Land. For here the Saviour was born. He worked, lived and rose again in this land. His church reached its years of discretion in Jerusalem and through countless dramas that shaped the land's history the church wove its design, often falteringly, but with eternity in it. Consequently, the new Israel is a living museum with exhibitions of the church's varied history—the old petrified monuments to the early church's dogmatic conflicts, the Greek church in its changing nuances, Roman Catholicism's powerful activity and nearly all the Protestant sects. But the Christians are practically speaking all Arabs, some 50,000 in all, while the Jewish Christians are so few that they can be counted on one's fingers. For Israel is the Jews' country, its official religion Judaism. And when a Christian mission seeks admittance, sparks from the clash between synagogue and church fly once again.

Since the establishment of the State of Israel, a remarkable number of Christian missionaries have come to the country. Orthodox Jews called it a veritable offensive. The first result has been a violent reaction by the Jews. They have begun to organise a counter-offensive and are endeavouring to enlist the support of the authorities. They claim that certain foreign missions, especially some rather business-minded American missionaries, use underhand means and try to 'purchase' souls in return for food parcels and clothes. Or they tempt people with promises of visas for countries where conditions are less austere than they are in Israel—but the stipulated terms are baptism.

Clearly, however, no one need fear such actions, which do not affect the spirit, while people who can be bought are no loss. It looks worse from the Christian angle, but, there again, there is no need to waste many words on the small numbers concerned; only to say that they are not a good advertisement for Christianity.

What is important is that Israel feels she needs a breathing-space. This small nation has been through so many violent crises that it is incapable of thinking about new ones. And the absorption of vast masses of immigrants from a diversity of countries requires that state and people must concentrate on unification. Because of this, the Israelis find it unfair that Christian missions should create new divisions at this time and urge them to wait for a decade or two.

There is religious liberty in Israel, and Christian missionaries are free to operate there, within certain limits, at any rate, and they are also protected by the authorities. But feelings towards them are far from friendly and they should beware of provocative behaviour.

And with this provisionally last phase in the two thousand years' conflict between synagogue and church, we must now attempt a final evaluation of the relationship between the two.

THERE IS A STORY ABOUT HOW THE FIRST
railway was planned between Moscow and St.
Petersburgh, as Leningrad was then called. The
engineers gave the Tsar their views about the route the line
ought to follow. It should be determined by the terrain, as
formed by rivers, the condition of the soil and hills, and
provide the small communities en route with connections
with the big towns. Then the railway would be like an old
natural road that winds through the landscape and as a result
of thousands of years of tradition creates an intimate en-
semble with nature, road and human settlements all playing
their part. But the Tsar shook his head; he put a ruler on
the map and drew a straight line from Moscow to St. Petersburgh. 'The line shall look like this,' he said. And it did.

Modern road-building follows the Tsar's ruler. The road
cuts brutally through hills and is raised above depressions on
embankments. Where old roads wind in charming curves
and avoid steep gradients and sudden descents, following
the level alongside rivers and connecting places where men
live, the asphalt road majestically makes its way through or
above the obstacles it meets. Man is stronger than nature
and proves it once again here.

All too often the spectacle of spiritual life resembles a
modern motorway. A ruler is used to draw a line which cuts
through straight as an arrow and rejects what others believe
and think. The riddle of life is proclaimed solved. Here is
the answer to all questions, and light on mysteries men are

generally silent about. For thousands of years synagogue and church considered and judged each other as if by the ruler. The synagogue knew that the Christian faith was blasphemy; the church declared that the Jews were cursed by God. There could be no question of negotiation; one was white, the other black. And neither of the two adversaries has yet quite won free from this entangling web where prejudice and dogmatism determine all ideas.

But reality smiles at the two obdurate and self-righteous opponents and leaves them behind. For there are facts that talk another language. They say that that which is spirit and has eternity in it finds its own ways. And the ways of the spirit are surprising; they seldom follow the straight line of cold logic and cannot be controlled by an electronic brain. We have briefly followed the two ways which carried Judaism and Christianity for millennia and seen that they twisted forward and were built where no one else saw a way, and brought both the chosen people and God's church across the swamp and through untold dangers. We are silent in the face of the mysterious fact that they both survived when they ought to have succumbed according to all the laws of common sense.

This is the crux of everything that this book has to say. We see two religions confronting each other both of which sprang from the same root and profess one God, the Creator, the Redeemer, and bow to His holy will. And this one almighty God chose Israel as His people. He revealed himself and made a covenant with them. Israel needs no one else and has clung to Him for thousands of years. But this same living God led its history by winding ways so that in the middle of it—we Christians say 'in the fulness of time'—He gave His Son to redeem us through suffering and death; He raised him from the dead and made a new covenant with the world. Israel said 'no' to it and the church 'yes'; the two parted and God's one way became two ways which eventually ran far apart.

The previous chapters have told the stories of Israel during its long wandering and of the church during its shorter, but also lengthy wandering. We have felt ashamed of the blood that flowed and the injustice the strong showed the weak, with tears and despair as consequences; we have listened to fiery uncontrolled quarrels of the kind that often explode among relatives. But the question remains: which of the two found the right way? Or: has God given men two ways to salvation, one via Sinai for Israel, the other from Golgotha for everyone else, but both ways hastening towards the same heaven?

It is easy to ask—but how is an answer possible when we dare to look into the Almighty's secret thoughts and plans. So we stop and let one of the Torah's wise sayings sink into our minds before we venture further: 'The hidden things are for the Lord our God, the revealed things for us and our children.' So we should humbly limit ourselves to considering the little God wants to reveal to his inquisitive creatures and abstain from empty guesswork. As the iceberg in the deep hides by far the greatest part of itself and only lets a tenth show above the surface, so it is with eternal life. But I also believe that God smiles on the man who never tires in his attempt to follow and study 'the revealed things', i.e. the footsteps He has left behind in the course of history —especially where Israel, the apple of his eye, and the church that believes in His son are concerned.

And the first revealed thing is that Jesus Christ stands at the division between the two. The church misused his name so often that the synagogue does not even possess a niche in which to put him alongside Israel's other great men. But for Christians he bears the name above all names. Earlier on we established, and it still holds good, that everyone must make his personal choice with regard to Jesus. Here the ways part. The Jew is a Jew; the Christian is a Christian. The difference between the two is so fundamental and clear-cut that no one should try to obliterate it or explain it away. Superficial goodwill and a friendly clap on the back serve no

purpose. Tolerance is a fine word, but it must not be confused with lukewarmness where one's own convictions are
concerned. No, the two come closest, if the Jew is a true
Jew and the Christian is a Christian in the strongest sense
of the word. Only then can they help each other to find the
answer to the great questions.

Naturally there are people on both sides who are never
at a loss for an answer and do not even need to think before
it pops out of their mouths. A strictly orthodox Christian,
who accepts Christianity's absolute and unique truth without compromise, is bound to tremble at the very thought of
leaving the Jews in peace from Christian missions. And the
Jew who passes a crucifix on the road and whispers at the
figure on the cross, '*Yemach shemo,* May his name be obliterated', is in the same boat as the Christian.

Answers of that kind remind us of modern motorways
that run on impatient of restraint and refuse to be blocked,
however steep or deep the obstacle, but settle every problem
by drawing a line with a ruler. Spirit does not tolerate such
heavy-handed behaviour. It punishes by withdrawing itself
and leaving the man who was secure behind in darkness.
We remember how we discovered in the picture in the
church that the woman who symbolised the church was just
as blind as the one who represented the synagogue, and had
a bandage over her eyes too.

The way to the answer is long and not as straight as most
people believe, for 'the revealed things' determine its course.
And the revealed things are hills and chasms—or, to use another word, facts, of the kind we found time and again in
the history of both church and synagogue.

We have followed the two sister religions step by step.
We saw the first one grow to middle age and the younger
develop in the shelter of the elder. We listened when dis-
cord began to jar and saw the crack open that was soon to
gape wide. The ways parted and led far apart, but never so
far that they forgot each other. For countless bonds link them
together and neither of them ever frees itself from the other.

o

Both have survived the millennia. The synagogue went through ordeals by fire more scorching than those experienced by any other people, at times mortally wounded, but always saved in the end. And even though the church was split up into innumerable communities and sects, and apathy and indecision and worldliness caused much that was once green to wither, it is as alive today as it was nearly two thousand years ago.

Synagogue and church—both kept alive by the Eternal himself, He who is the secret, the mystery, hidden in both of them. So they are links in His plan; He has need of them both. Faced with such facts, neither Jew nor Christian should cling blindly to his own religion and condemn the other, still less use his strength to convince the man who is already convinced and make him reject what life for many generations has confirmed as coming from God.

No, we are forced to face the next choice and are confronted with a paradox: that the Almighty is One and His Truth absolute. And yet He gave the synagogue one part of His light and the church another part. And the two lights sometimes shine in different ways and vie with one another. Here everyone must make a choice.

It is easiest for the man who is content to stare at one side of the paradox—his own—and draw a line striking out the other.

It is truer and more realistic to accept the paradox and its tension in one's mind and realise that oneself and everything that one does not comprehend is hidden in God.

There is one definite prerequisite before Jew and Christian can view one another with respect and meet in free and frank discussions so that both reap some benefit. The Jew, as we saw Franz Rosenzweig do, must concede Christianity its place in God's household, and the Christian discover, I repeat discover, because Christian teaching has always stifled the mere possibility of envisaging it, that the Jew's way, like his own, is made by God and the two ways lead to the same heaven.

Two ways. The simile of religions as ways is old. The New Testament uses it sometimes when it talks about salvation in Christ. The Gospel according to St. John mentions a saying of Jesus, in which he calls himself the way and in the Acts of the Apostles the way simply means the Gospel and belief in it. There is also a saying that points out two ways, the broad one leading to destruction and the narrow one that leads to life. Like so much else in the New Testament, this allegory was taken from contemporary Jewish preaching. It is so vivid that we often find it developed and used in the early church. But if we compare the ways of synagogue and church, the image of a narrow and a broad way is valid in another sense. Success smiled on the church early and long, and that invited people to take the easy, broad way that many took. The synagogue, on the contrary, was always in the shadow of her younger sister; its way was narrow and only a few found it.

There is a story, which has no place in this book, that the Jews' wandering on this steep and stony way hardened them and developed qualities that we have grown used to calling Jewish. We emphasised one of them when we saw that their fight to win freedom and equality often drove them to adopt extremist attitudes, so that there have always been Jews in the left-wing of revolutionary circles. But the fight also made them pioneers in almost every branch of cultural life. The West would have been different and much poorer than it is without the Jewish contribution. This is often forgotten and has never been appreciated as it deserves to be. We must also be content merely to point out the equally neglected fact that both ways come to a halt before the enormous Asian mountain range, whose highest peaks are the Himalayas. Apart from a few scattered attempts, neither synagogue nor church ever climbed it and reached the Far East to try their strength against its ancient religions. Islam, the far younger sister of Israel and the church, succeeded in their stead, and there is neither time nor space for us to compare the two with Islam here. We simply take a passing glance at these loose ends, which others can take up and follow, and turn back to the broad and narrow ways of church and synagogue.

For many centuries the church surged powerfully forward along its broad way. In the West Christianity and culture were synonymous. Slender church towers and steeples marked the silhouettes of towns and villages; the chiming of bells mingled with the sound of everyday life; the church formed the framework for festivals at life's milestones. Admittedly, unbelief, doubt and opposition existed, but seldom, practically never, in open concrete form. What the church stamped as unbelief was doubt about Christian dogmas or defiance of the decisions and policy of the princes of the church. And when rabbis and priests disputed their faiths, or Martin Luther challenged Rome with his theses, half Europe followed the conflict on tenterhooks.

Much of this has disappeared. Recent centuries have effected a change in the spiritual climate; interest in religious problems has cooled. The images of a mighty Jehovah and the bleeding, crucified Galilean faded long ago. Not that war is waged on synagogue and church in the West—that is left to the Iron Curtain countries—but religious questions have disappeared from the general public's range of interests. Why discuss which religion is the right one, when they may all be equally right and equally wrong, and it does not matter if it is one or the other, for none of them is of any interest?

A well-known rabbi in Detroit told me that to many Jews in the city Judaism was like a grandmother. They visited her four times a year, took care not to contradict her and had not the heart to do anything they knew would distress her. In another town I mentioned this comment to a rabbi I met and he remarked that the comparison was very much to the point, but that it was not worded sharply enough. In his experience Judaism was not a grandmother, but a great-grandmother. People had heard of her, but never seen her. If this description applies to American Jews, it is equally valid for European Christians.

This means that now the church can prepare itself to share the lot of the synagogue. The broad way has narrowed. In this new period which can be called post-Jewish and post-Christian, both ways are narrow and the fact that they are moving out to the periphery does not impoverish either Jews or Christians; faith and success have no connection with each other. And God, who governs the course of history, also has his intentions here.

But Christians are learning to read the Bible in a way they have not known since the church's early days. A great deal of it acquires a brand-new significance. A phrase such as 'a remnant of Israel', the 7,000 who did not bend the knee to Baal, seems more valuable when Christians realise that now it concerns their church too. Just as the Jews were in *galut* for thousands of years, the Christians are pilgrims and strangers on the earth, and the expression 'the invisible church', *ecclesia invisibilis*, has more point than ever before.

I wonder if the idea behind this is that difficult times will teach synagogue and church to look ahead to the things that are to come? Here in any case is what unites them and helps them to come closer together. After all, they are both waiting for one who is to come, the Jews for Messiah, the Christians for the return of Jesus, and the two are the same person. Jews and Christians can pray together: 'Thy kingdom come.'

Philology tells us that the word 'way' is akin to the Latin *vehere*, to carry, draw, and the Old English *weg*, to move or journey. In other words, a way is not defined as something to stand still on. In itself the way is a dead thing; it stays where it is laid. But it is intended for movement. We talk of being on our way, and the way *runs* through the countryside. When this book calls Judaism and Christianity two ways, the reason is that they are built and made by God, and we can look back and study them as they wind through the landscapes of history down the millennia. They began in the distant past and twisted between hill and dale; bridges carried them over rivers and gorges and it is truly enlightening to discover how they never allowed themselves to be stopped or ran out into the sands of the desert and disappeared, but were always—*on their way*!

But religions are not merely historical facts or dead things. The purpose behind them is not realised until men travel by way of them and move forward. Religion is more than a subject for study; it is first and foremost for use, to live in. Until men move in it, it has no life of its own. And Jews and Christians have wandered along the two ways; they shall do so as long as the earth exists.

And away on the far horizon, beyond the hills and further than the eye can see, where heaven and earth meet each other, the two ways shall meet the same Lord and become one. On that day, they will no longer be ways—they will have reached the goal.

BIBLIOGRAPHY

BIBLIOGRAPHY

Leo Baeck: *Judaism and Christianity*. London, 1954.

Morris Goldstein: *Jesus in Jewish Tradition*. New York, 1960.

Malcolm Hay: *The Foot of Pride*. Boston, 1951.

Göte Hedenquist: *The Church and the Jewish People*. London, 1954.

R. Travers Herfort: *Pharisaism*. London, 1912; *Christianity in Talmud and Midrash*. London, 1903.

Jocz, J.: *The Jewish People and Jesus Christ*. London, 1954; *A Theology of Election*. London, 1958.

Henry Enoch Kagan: *Changing the Attitude of Christian towards Jew*. New York, 1952.

Joseph Klausner: *Jesus of Nazareth*. London, 1925; *From Jesus to Paul*. London, 1941.

George Foot Moore: *Judaism, 1-3*. Cambridge, 1950.

James Parkes: *The Conflict of the Church and the Synagogue*. Cleveland; *Judaism and Christianity*. London, 1948; *The Foundations of Judaism and Christianity*. London, 1960.

Michael Serafian: *The Pilgrim*. New York, 1964.

Hans Joachim Schoeps: *The Jewish-Christian Argument*. New York, 1963.

Abba Hillel Silver: *Where Judaism Differed*. New York, 1956.

INDEX

INDEX

215